I GUESS I'M A DAD NOW:

A HUMOROUS HANDBOOK FOR NEW-ISH DADS WHO DON'T WANT TO SUCK

CORY JENKS

Edited by: Rumki Chowdhury

Proofread by: Jveria Gauhar

Cover photo credit: Todd Helmick

Cover design: Khizra Saeed

Production Services: Global Bookshelves International, LLC
Images of Cory's children were used with the permission of Cory and Cassie Jenks.

Printed in the United States of America.

To comment on this book, email cory@improvrx.com.

Note: The author has made every effort to ensure the accuracy and completeness of the information presented in this book. However, the author cannot be held responsible for the continued currency of the information or any inadvertent errors. Therefore, the author shall have no liability to any person or entity with regard to claims, loss, or damage caused or alleged to be caused, directly or indirectly, by the use of the information contained herein. The author would like to remind the readers (especially his family) that he is a comedian and writes to inform *and* make people laugh. It might be a good idea right now to remember the importance of taking a joke. On second thought, even if I am not related to you, please know nothing in this book was written out of spite, anger, or rage. Rather, an attempt to educate on a very heavy topic with a dose of humor. If you encounter anything that makes you wonder if you should laugh or get angry with me. Choose laughter.

I Guess I'm a Dad Now: A Humorous Handbook for New-Ish Dads Who Don't Want to Suck -- 1st ed.

ISBN (Paperback): 9798990258303
eISBN: 9798990258310

Dedication

To all those dads doing your best out there: Hang in there; you can do this!

To my kids: I'd thank you for making me a dad, but that was really "the work" your mom and I put in. Make sure you think about that, especially once you hit puberty.

To Dad: You may not have passed down your speed, hand-eye coordination, or jump shot, but you passed down something much more useful: how to raise a kid right.

Table of Contents

like our sea levels and curious nationwide love of the Dallas Cowboys. I am not telling you this to scare you. Rather, to show you that we, as dads (and possible future dads if you are kidless and reading this), have a lot on our shoulders. Reading these dire statistics may make it sound like we have an impossible task in front of us. That there is nothing that we can do to make a dent in society's major problems. That it would take a superhuman to be a dad who can make a difference.

Well, I have good news for you:

The bar to be a decent dad has never been lower. Look around. No, really, if you are in public, put this book down and look around. Thanks to our obsession with mobile devices, social media, and the legalization of online betting, most dads you are observing are probably emotionally distant from their kids, faces buried in a screen, and hands full of some sort of sugary, salty, fatty snack (or a fancy can of a microbrew if you are in Denver).

The reality is that if you are reading a book on parenting (like the one in your hands right now), you already are, or are going to be, a great dad. It shows that you care. It shows that you are willing to make an effort. It shows that you are willing to learn.[2]

And how about some *good* statistics to show how being a *present* dad can make a positive impact on the world?

- Finland is the only country where fathers spend more time with school-age children than mothers do, clocking in on an average 8 minutes more on

---

2   *If you are not yet a parent and are reading this book, please put it down and go to a movie. Or take a random trip. DO IT WHILE YOU HAVE THE FREEDOM.*

childcare than mothers.[3]

- Eighty-five percent of fathers consider being a dad "the best job in the world."[4] And in all fairness, the other 15% are probably video game testers, ice cream tasters, and/or the Hawaiian Tropic "oil boys" that Harry and Lloyd from *Dumb and Dumber* referred the bus-full-of-models to at the end of the movie.

- Finally, 62% of dads are hungry for more information on how they can be a better dad for their kids.[4] And the other 38%? They aren't reading this book!

I will soon get into a little bit more about who I am and why you'd even listen to me on parenting, or specifically, fatherhood advice. This book is just one of many resources to help dads be better at being dads. At the end of this book, I will list several of these, which I have turned to during my dadding journey. These people are much more intelligent than I am and have done much more clinical research on the subject of parenting than I have.

However, I can speak from experience: what has worked for me and what hasn't. I have also read some advice that I thought was downright counterproductive and dumb. How do I know this? Besides our look around at the absent-minded, distracted, and possibly intoxicated dads, have you been around kids much these days? Have you seen how these kids turn into teenagers? Have you seen

3   Source: https://childhood-central.com/state-of-the-worlds-fathers-30-statistics-on-fatherhood/
4   Source: https://parentspluskids.com/blog/fatherhood-statistics-trends-and-analysis

how these teenagers turn into adults?

Yikes!

Things are not looking too pretty for our current (2023 as I write this) generation of young adults. While I may be suffering from a bit of "in my day, my generation was better" syndrome, I think the current crop of new adults struggle with communication, focus, and work ethic. I don't think we, Millennials, are any better because we struggle with many of the same, if not similar, issues as our Generation Alpha kids. One of the reasons? How we were raised.

I think, too often, parenting books miss the point that the goal isn't to raise good kids, but capable (and tax-paying, not collecting) adults. When bad dads create bad kids, those same bad kids turn into bad adults. Bad adults who are rude when serving food at a restaurant, can't listen to a problem at work, or are even unwilling to do any sort of hard work.

Did I mention there is a lot at stake with being a dad?

There are a lot of good intentions in parenting books, parenting advice columns, and the "too many to count" blogs that pepper the internet. But did you know what the road to hell is paved with? Good intentions. So, I am making sure my intentions are clear with this book:

They are selfish.

I want to live in a world where I don't see checked-out dads checking in on their fantasy football scores while their kids are begging for their attention at the park.

I want to live in a world where kids don't take their resentment for their father out on their boss (who may just be me someday).

I want to live in a world full of happy, tax-paying citizens, who have a healthy relationship with their dad, are competent in their endeavors, and are at least tolerable to interact with.

I will admit these are lofty, selfish goals. But it starts with you, Dad.

At this point, if you are still reading, I will take a short break to introduce myself and explain why you would even want to listen to me. From there, I will lay out the goal of the book so you can decide if you want to keep reading or if you are still in the Amazon free return window. Don't worry. You won't hurt my feelings. I have toddlers that already do that multiple times a day.

Oh yes, who am I? If you failed to read the cover of the book, my name is Cory. At the time of this writing, I am a mid-30s dude who grew up in Tucson, Arizona, attempting, but often failing at playing many sports, mostly baseball, basketball, racquetball, and golf. After I finished high school, I said, "to hell with this town." I went out to get my doctor of pharmacy degree, a PharmD (that's right, I am technically a "doctor," but I don't make anyone refer to me as that...except for the jerks that were assholes to me in high school. You know who you are (Adam) at the University of South Carolina. I am a proud Gamecock. And yes, I do love adorning my kids in clothes that say, "Cocks." Sorry if that offends you; it's my alma mater. And please refer to me as "doctor."

After college, I said, "To hell with this town (Columbia, SC—a lovely place, but it wasn't for me)," and made a *mea culpa* with Tucson, came back, then met my wife.

6

She is a nurse practitioner, and we joke that together, we make "almost one real doctor." Speaking of my wife, she is an amazing mother, but it wasn't always that way. No, not that she was a bad mother; we just waited a while to have kids. Man, that DINK (dual income, no kids) life was pretty sweet. We traveled. We got deep into hobbies. We developed meaningful friendships. What was I talking about? Oh yeah, being a dad. It's tiring and not always rewarding. I mean, it's great. It's totally great 1000% of the time.

Before we had our first kid in 2018 (checks birth certificate to confirm), as I mentioned, we got deep into hobbies. One of mine was improv comedy. Yes, I am a pharmacist *and* a comedian. Oh, and an author. Not just the author of this book. I published a book on my use of comedy *in* healthcare in 2022 called, *Permission to Care: Building a Healthcare Culture that Thrives in Chaos.* Have you read it? Based on my sales data, you most likely have not.

Anyway, it turns out I like writing, and the short list of people who read my last book liked reading it. And if you can believe it, writing a book did not make me want to stop writing books; instead, it made me want to write *more.* Lucky for you, right?

Along those comedic background lines, I should disclose that this will not be some stuffy, "holier than thou" kind of book on parenting. There are enough of those books around. My goal is to filter some of the best lessons I have learned and applied in my first five years of parenting to help you, intrepid father, have a more enjoyable, smooth parenting experience. As I already mentioned, I will point you toward some really amazing fatherhood and parenting resources. Because one of the best lessons I can pass along as a dad is to know your limits.

I am not a parenting expert.

But I do have a few things going for me:

- Five years' experience raising kids
- A comedic filter to make reading this book as (hopefully) enjoyable as possible
- Two kids that other adults willingly babysit and invite to their events and a brand new third kid, who the jury is still out on if others will tolerate

And I think that the final point is what should catch your attention. While I did start this book with an entire diatribe about raising adults, we can't forget about being able to enjoy the journey while they are kids. Part of that is having kids others enjoy (or tolerate) being around (at least for now). So far, my wife and I have passed that test.

This book will be a compilation of my observations, experiences, and tricks to help you along the various paths of fatherhood so you, too, can enjoy the company of others with your kids, while also being able to enjoy life *occasionally* without your kids, if you can find people willing to watch them.

A quick note on perspectives. This book will be written from my perspective and experiences on parenting two boys (our newest addition is a girl, so look for the book's next edition, where I have to update all of my advice) up to around age five. I don't claim to know what the hell to do when dadding a ten-year-old or a (*shudders*) teenager.

Those are for my next edition(s). I cover the "pre-kid phase," and the advice I share, in no particular order, by the way, is for those early years. I am also married. So, for those divorced and single dads rockin' it, while I still think you can find a lot of what I say useful, know that I have never been in your shoes. If I miss something or say something that doesn't apply to you, I'm sorry. Remember, as I said earlier, it is important to know your limits.

Another note on perspective. I am a white dude (and fairly a-religious). My mom is Jewish, and my dad is Methodist. We celebrated some Jewish holidays growing up and had a Christmas tree in our house. My high school friends called me "Rabbi Jenks," and we have our kids in a Christian daycare (take that for what it's worth). Also, I was raised in a middle-class household, living in the suburbs of Tucson. There is a *lot* I can't pretend to know about other races, cultures, and socioeconomic statuses, and probably an entire list of things that I am missing. Again, I will try to make this advice as universal as possible, but know that if I come off as tone-deaf, it's more from a lack of experience. So, let me apologize in advance and know I am doing my best.

A final note on perspective. When I first thought about writing a parenting book, it would be just that: a "parenting" book. After some contemplation, I realized I was a dude. Therefore, my perspective probably wouldn't fit well for moms. Not to say moms won't buy (please buy!), read, and learn from this book. But I wanted to focus on the guys. Because it's what I know. When I was discussing this book idea with a family member (I will keep the name anonymous, but let's just say it came from the "in-laws" side), I was told the idea of writing a book for dads was "sexist." I politely nodded while they said this and immediately ignored their terrible advice. Because I think we, dudes, need something different just for, well, us. We are different; we offer different evolutionary skill sets, and how else was I going to make fun of my wife if I didn't write a book specifically NOT for wives?! Now, she'll never know!

I hope you decide to take this ride with me as I discuss what has worked, what hasn't worked, and what can make your experience as a dad more enjoyable. Because even though the work is hard, it doesn't mean it can't be fun along the way. And while I can't promise the act of *being* a dad will be as fun as the act of *making* yourself a dad[5] (wink wink), I still think that you'll be able to find a lot of joy along the way.

---

5   *My mom likes to remind me about how "hard" it was to make me, and how long it took, and how much "work" it was. Here's my first tip-maybe, when you are a parent, don't bring up the "origin story" as it could just ruin sex for your kids. On second thought, make sure you bring it up a lot once they hit puberty. It could be the verbal equivalent of spraying cold water on a dog in heat.*

Chapter 1

To Breed or Not to Breed? That Is the Question

Perhaps this book has gotten into your hands before it's too late. I mean, before you decided to take the joyful, never hard, and always rewarding step of becoming a parent. And maybe you are on the fence about having kids. The fact that you are even putting some thought into dadding and reading a book shows you have enough introspection to make the right choice for you.

And that last word is the most key: *you*. The choice has to be right for you. Now when I say "you," I mean the "royal you" and whoever will let you fornicate with them. For a very long time, my wife and I did not want kids. She was in graduate school. I was enjoying the free time and hobbies that had eluded me through pharmacy school and residency. But even once my wife was out of grad school, living that DINK life was sweet!

Cassie and I on our wedding day, January 3rd, 2014.
A good four years before kids. So happy. So free. So
clueless.

Even on our honeymoon to Maui, we met a couple in their 40s with no kids who were living a great life. They had several nieces and nephews, a full bank account, and zero regrets. As my wife started feeling the tingles and jingles in her empty uterus, I tried to remind her of the couple from Maui. How happy they seemed. How relaxed. How...free.

If you can't tell, I was not quite as ready to create human life as my wife was. So I cut her a pretty awesome deal: if the Cubs won the World Series, we could try and have kids. It had been 108 years since they had been able to pull it off, and they were historically inept. I thought that my freedom, sanity, and money were safe.

Let's just say there were more than just tears of joy when they won it all in 2016.

Alright, my kids might read this someday and think I didn't want them. That's not true. I just wanted to ensure a very statistically low chance that we'd have them. (If you are reading, kids, I'd pay for your therapy, but you already took my prime years and money away from me. If you want to fix whatever issues you have, it's up to you to pay for it.)

Sorry, back to the reasons to (or not to) have kids. As my wife and I were starting to see our friends procreate, there began to come some, how do I say this nicely, pressure. It came from friends, from family, and from society at large. Below, I will list some of the reasons that people "think" they should have kids. I'll explain why it's a terrible list shortly:

- "We want grandkids!"
- "Babies are so cute."
- "It's sooooo rewarding."
- "Maybe it will fix whatever is wrong in our

relationship?"

- "It will help us focus on those habits we need to change."

If I missed other "reasons" that people have given you to have kids, please let me know (preferably not in an angry, but rather, kind email or review), and I will throw them in the next edition. And I will give YOU the credit! Helping other dads and getting famous, ...how's that for a deal?

In reality, I want to explain to you the problems that having kids solve and the ones that having kids don't solve to better guide you toward your decision.

Here are the problems having kids solve: not having kids.

Here are the problems kids don't solve: everything else.

The problem they do solve is pretty self-explanatory, so let's dive into what creating little humans *doesn't* solve.

"We want grandkids!"

Oh, your parents and possibly in-laws have had an empty nest for too long. They want to know that their decision to have you and your "kid-havin' partner" will result in a genetic victory for them by having their DNA passed down to another generation. Plus, all of *their* friends' kids have already had kids and made them grandparents. And they don't want to be the only ones without those precious grandkids.

I admit that both my parents and in-laws are very loving with our kids. And we are lucky enough to live in the same city, so they get to be a part of their grandkids' lives a lot. For that, we and our kids are grateful and fortunate. However...

Remember who will take care of your kids when they are up sick in the middle of the night. Or throwing a tantrum while refusing to get in the car to go to school. Or who insists you buy them more of that slightly more expensive version of food because they "love it," only to refuse it the next day. Or who gets featured on the news when their kids become a Russian asset and start selling military secrets while selling out Uncle Sam.

You will be. Not the grandparents.

While, if you are lucky, they will be a wonderful and possibly helpful part of your kids' lives, it is still you on the hook for it. And take heed of what happened to me. For years, my mother, in all her Jewish guilt, kept asking if we were going to change our minds about kids. Eventually, the asking became nagging, and then, thanks to a Ben Zobrist 10th-inning single and my deal with my wife: we had our first son. She was happy. We were, too, but also, we were handling the lion's share of the "raising kids" part.

Fast forward to a few years later, and we explained to her we were contemplating an unprecedented third kid. Instead of the "I need grandkids" excitement from years earlier, the reaction was, "You are already pretty tired. Are you sure you can handle another?"

Um, thanks for the advice?

Having kids for the sake of your parents is kind of like giving your kids exactly what they ask for. At first, they'll love you and be excited, but then, the shine of any new thing wears off. Even grandkids, apparently.[6]

Ultimately, having kids should be about satisfying *your* own desire to pass on your DNA, not anyone else's, not even your parents.

"Babies are so cute."

I won't deny this one, only with the caveat that *some* babies are so cute. Some are decidedly less so. With all due respect and apologies to my second son, Henry, when he came out of his mom, I don't think he was done cooking yet. He really looked more like an alien than a cute human baby. Maybe, it's an unfair comment, considering he earned himself an immediate trip to the Neonatal Intensive Care Unit for a day, but the kiddo wasn't that cute out of the uterus. Cut to three months later, and he was well on his way to being a handsome baby lady killer.

Even for those babies that come out of the womb looking fresh, fly, and cute as hell, there are a couple of sobering realities to remember:

- Cuteness will not predict a lack of getting up in the middle of the night to take care of them.
- Cuteness will not keep them from turning into toddlers that melt down, ruin plans, and generally destroy any nice piece of clothing/furniture/automobile you have.
- Cuteness eventually gets a surge of hormones that renders them moody, angry, and obstinate

---

6   *My mother is a wonderful grandmother to our kids, I love her, they love her, and we are grateful for her. And one of the things we love her for is her honesty. And she wasn't lying, I was and am pretty tired. Now I am tired with three kids.*

from a book. While I am entertaining, and I have some awesome kids, I am not a parenting expert in the academic sense. But as a pharmacist, I am trained to say, "I don't know," a lot, especially when someone tries to show me a rash in their groin area. Thankfully, those same "defer to the expert" skills carry over to my author style. So, in the back is an appendix of books and resources to help you and your kids along the way. How do I know they will help? I don't know, but here's to hoping they will because they are the same ones that helped me and my wife.

So, You've Decided to Build Your Army?

One thing you can expect when you're expecting your first kid is people asking if you want to have more. I can remember being asked, "So, is this it, or are you going to try for more?" almost before the amniotic fluid had dried on my first kid after their exit from my wife's uterus. People don't have much tact, as having kids has taught me. But as I said about the kid shamers, the number you wish to have (or at least try to have; sorry to those wanting one and getting twins on your first shot) is up to you.

So, how do you know how many you want? This is an answer that only you can know. And by you, I mean the mother of your kids, because we aren't the ones growing a bowling ball in our gut for nine months only to try and push it out between our thighs, for which the reward is months of that bowling ball, latched onto our nipples. Personally, I never saw myself having three kids. That was primarily due to the fact that in high school and college, I never dreamed I would actually have the opportunity to have sex three times. But once I found myself a willing partner, and we decided to add kids to the equation, the conversations went as follows:

After the first kid.

Me: Wow, he's great! I think it would be hard to top Jake. Having kids is a big risk, and why roll the dice again?

My wife: Who will he play with? He needs a sibling.

Me: I was essentially an only child since my sister moved out when I was 11, and it was the happiest seven years of my childhood.

My wife: We're having two.

After the second kid.

Me: Wow, Henry is amazing, but that trip to the NICU was a bit too much for me. I can't imagine going through that again. Plus, we'd be outnumbered.

My wife: I'm not ready to be done yet. Plus, I had THREE other siblings, and we loved it.

Me: You weren't the ones raising you hellions.

My wife: Remember when you thought having sex three times was out of your reach? You're getting closer.

Me: Three kids sound great! Let's try right now.

As you can see, we had a very exact science when it came to choosing the number of kids. I think the science says I trust my wife, and I am happy to go along for the ride. But as I type this, with three kids, we are both firmly in the "we're done" camp. It feels great being on the same page and knowing we have no desire to have enough kids for a basketball team.

Other people I have talked to had grand plans for more kids and then, after their first one came along quickly, did an about-face and said vehemently, "Hell no! We're not doing that again!" They are happy parents of one kid.

I have a friend who, along with his wife, decided on four kids before they were married. First of all, kudos on the planning. Secondly, double kudos on willingly being double-outnumbered. Although, I do respect his approach. It is sort of like Odysseus lashing himself to this ship's mast so that the sirens' songs couldn't veer him off course. No matter how many late nights, dirty diapers, and skinned knees my friend's first three kids have, they are going for four. As of now, they are halfway there. I'll update you in this book's next edition, as I am sure you will be on pins and needles for years.

On the other hand, I might have veered too much in the "let the mom decide" on the number of kids. It really does need to be a team choice because if you, Dad, want more kids, but Mom doesn't, there could be some serious resentment. And vice versa. If Mom just needs to have a gaggle that can play four square together, but you really felt like three was the right number, you might secretly resent that fourth kid. Therefore, raising kids is best done as a team-based approach. I'll elaborate more on adding new team members next, but the most important team choice is getting on the same page with how many little hellions you want to try to bring into this world and raise together.

Lean on Me

When it comes to being a dad, the bad news is that you won't know everything. That's why you are reading a book from an "expert" like me, right? But it's not just about how to change a diaper, burp a fussy baby, or not leave frozen breast milk out by accident.[11] Appliances, furniture, and toys around your house are going to break. You are going to want to build something you don't have a tool for. Your washer will flood your house, and you'll need to know if you *really* need those full mitigation procedures they are insisting you need (we didn't). Even if you *are* handy, a great gardener, or know how to spot a crooked home repair company, having kids is going to drain your energy and attention. My experience as a dad juggling kids, house projects, and book-writing is well summed up in the 311 song *Don't Tread on Me*:

"I'm not trying to be perfect, just get one damn thing done."

I used to try and be perfect at everything, such is my pharmacist brain. Now, I lean on my network as much as possible. As the old saying goes, "It takes a village." Usually, that is finished with, "To raise a child." However, I'd like to revise that last line by saying, "To keep a Dad sane." Here are a few of the people I lean on in my network:

✗Construction project question guy: I have a friend who is a contractor who builds custom homes. When I needed to add a gate to my fence or close a hole in my wall to close off a room, I asked him what he thought, and in the case of the gate, to help me. He has two kids

---

11   *Your partner will likely make your murder look like an "accident" if you leave any of that precious white gold out and ruin it after it's been pumped. I am barely alive to write this book. Thankfully my wife showed me mercy after I let a few bags of her frozen breastmilk thaw in the garage accidentally.*

of his own, so any bigger project goes to whoever he recommends. Gotta respect his time too.

🌳Yardwork: I got a whole crew for this. Not a hired work crew. If I need some mulch moved around my yard, I ask the neighboring kids. Need a tree trimmed and chipped? That's my father-in-law. Want to know how best to install my garden? Oh, I got an urban farmer guy. How to trim those trees? Oh, you know I got a tree guy.

🏠Real Estate: Not only is our real estate agent a great friend, but he is also a *really good* agent with a ton of rental properties. He helped us find our dream home in a dream neighborhood and is helping us along the rental real estate world. He also knows a ton of reliable contractors for those projects my construction guy is too busy for. Oh, and he took the picture for the cover of this book, too. Maybe he should be my "Renaissance Man Guy."

🔥Fires: Yeah, my friend is a firefighter. I live in the desert. Things can go sideways real quick. Always good to bounce my bonfire plans off him beforehand.

🗡Nutrition: This is more a hybrid of online resources, books, a pharmacist friend who is deep down the rabbit hole of the healthiest way of eating, and a friend of ours who puts on a health and nutrition conference. I'll talk more about feeding your kids later.

📇 Pediatric Medication Dosing: A previous pharmacy professor is on my list of contacts and is always willing to respond to a text with a medication dosing question. At this point, you're wondering, "Aren't you a pharmacist? Can't you dose meds?" I can, but when it's *your own* kid, a second (smarter) opinion is always warranted, especially when you have been up all night and aren't thinking as straight as you'd like to. There is the crying. The incessant coughing. The occasional vomiting. And that's just from us parents. Sick kids will make you do dumb things, and with medicine, you may only get one shot at getting your kid(s) to take it, so it better be the right dose. When your eyes are bloodshot, your brain is foggy, and your kids are a nonstop factory of snot, tears, and insomnia, it never hurts to have a friend to lean on.

⌨Social Media: Oh, you liked my post? Thanks, but I didn't post it. I have an assistant for that. Nothing is a bigger waste of time than social media, so I compensate someone else to help me keep *my* most precious resource: time.

As you can see, it's nice to have people to lean on. My wife and I are also fortunate to have a lot of family near us that we can call on to help watch the kids, for example. If that is not you, build your network of child care. Our go-to babysitter is a friend of mine from my improv comedy days. There's no blueprint you have to follow. But having a network is a great way to make sure this parenting thing, which is already hard, need not be made harder by you trying to do everything yourself.

Create a "Silo of Sanity"

On the subject of building a team, let's talk about building something else that will help you keep it together on the Dad Path. Creating a cocoon of calm, a ring of reason, or as I like to call it, a "Silo of Sanity." In other words, it is important to have a group of friends, family, and media consumption that will help you stay sane in the wild sea of crazy that can invade your mind, body, and physical space.

Let me just say I realize I am coming from my own perspective, built on a life lived in basically two cities and at a single employer for the majority of my 11-year career, so I know I may have some blind spots. I am, as many of us are, in a silo. Instead of seeing it as a bad thing, I realized I have cultivated a "Silo of Sanity" between the media I consumed, the friends I made, and the neighbors I connected with. You need to insulate yourself from the insanity of most of society, lingering friends from past lives, and the family that you are stuck with who make or will make your job as a dad harder than it needs to be.

Now, I don't want to come off as some tin foil hat-wearing conspiracy theorist. But the reality is, whether it is on TV, at the movies, in commercials, or on your social media feed of choice, you are being sold a lot of stuff that is not helpful to your job of being the calm and steady presence of a dad. If you watch the news, it will tell you how things have never been worse, thereby captivating your undivided attention and taking every opportunity to show you how bad it is out there for your kid(s). I don't blame them; after all, they need eyeballs to watch them, their ads, and thus, make themselves lots of money. I have created my "Silo of Sanity" by not consuming much news at all.

While you may worry this will leave you "uninformed," I challenge you to really think about whenever the news gave you a life-changing bit of advice...that wasn't sponsored by a large food corporation or pharmaceutical company. The plus side of minimizing the news is minimizing advertisements. We are jumping ahead in the "practical tips" for raising toddlers, but when my boys and I watch TV, mostly to watch sports, they ask what commercials are and why there are so many getting in the way of watching the Cubs lose.

I'll let my oldest, five-year-old Jacob explain in his own words what Daddy has taught him:

"Commercials are just selling us stuff we don't need."

Whenever he says that, it's one of my proudest moments. My parents will push back and say that I "loved commercials" when I was a kid. I sure did, and our house had the Miracle Blade Perfection Series knives and Magic Bullet Blender to prove it.[12] My parents' approach to my media consumption may as well have been, "Set it and Forget it." So, if you are not careful, you will be at the whims of what the news and their commercials are trying to do to get you riled up while spending down your bank account.

Then there's social media, and I'm going to make this one brief: cleanse yourself of the negative energy and wasted time that comes with online trolls not worth your time. Unfriend, unfollow, and you know what's even

---

[12] *I will say that the Magic Bullet was one of the most entertaining/worst acted commercials I have ever seen. I still remember the guy who hated broccoli showing his delight when drinking the smoothie and exclaiming, "That tastes great, not like vegetables at all." Congratulations, Vernon! Don't believe me that this is some of the finest infomercials ever? Here are the best 28 minutes of your week. https://www.youtube.com/watch?v=w6KNpmRNyJM*

is not possible. Or it could mean a tougher conversation about how the behavior another family member's kids have on yours is not worth the time spent together.

Whether it's friends, family, or even a TV show that you don't want to influence your kids, I'll button this chapter up with my new take on the classic African proverb I expressed to you earlier. It has to do with remembering the most important thing(s) in your life (it's your kid(s), in case you weren't sure), and your job is to protect them and help them grow into the best version(s) of themselves as possible. With that being said, remember:

It may take a village to raise a child, but it only takes one village idiot to ruin them.

Chapter 3

Your Kid Will Fall Down

Alright, you've prepared your Silo of Sanity, are getting yourself in shape, and are assembling your Dad Assistance Network. You are going all in on having kids, and you are doing it for the right reason: you want kids. Awesome. Now it's time to face the daunting question you will inevitably be asked:

"You want to have a kid...in THIS world?"

Depending on whom you talk to, our current state of affairs in 2023 is some combination of the Salem Witch Trials, The Inquisition, and The (American) Civil War. Well, I got news for you. I am almost certain nobody who experienced those had central air conditioning while flying at 37,000 feet up in the air and having access to 70 million songs.[14] So, while society does have its problems, we also can have any food we want delivered with the touch of a button on our phone. It's no wonder we have an obesity crisis with the ease with which we can eat our feelings away.

On the other hand, I am not one of those blind optimists you may hear say things like, "The extra carbon in the atmosphere will actually help sustain 20 billion people on Earth" or "The good thing about antibiotic resistance is that it will motivate Big Pharma to create better medications." But I do think that if I could choose to live between right now and 100 years ago, I would say that for all its issues, 2023 is a more comfortable existence than 1923.

Therefore, if you are able to assuage the worries about the environment and antibiotic resistance, the next area of concern will likely be along the lines of, "But there are so many people, and it's so competitive. Aren't you worried about what your kid will grow up and do?" Now, it's no secret that artificial intelligence and automation are poised to disrupt our most tried and true jobs like drivin' trucks, luggin' trash, and operatin' on brain tumors. Just like the advent of the automobile created a huge market for gas stations, auto repair, and wacky, waving, inflatable-arm guys at used car lots, automation and AI (artificial intelligence) could create a whole new realm of jobs for the future.

---

14   *Thanks American Airlines for all of the choices, but if I get anywhere near listening to all of those, something has gone horribly wrong. On second thought, based on the number of delays and cancellations I have dealt with recently, 70 million may be light.*

Otherwise, our worst fears will be realized, and employment will look dramatically different and limited. At this time, I am going to lean on some fatherly wisdom my dad gave to me, which I ignored for too long. I hope that it sinks into you, your kids, as well as mine. Whenever I would get nervous about college admissions, residency matching, or finding a real pharmacist job, Ol' Mark (my dad's given first name) liked to tell me these three things:

1) Show up on time.

2) Work hard.

3) Be easy to work with.

My arguments usually were that I work in healthcare, and it's way different and more competitive than being a PE teacher like he was. Well, after over a decade of being a pharmacist, I have to say that Dad was right. I'd give him more credit, but he doesn't read books, so anything I write would be lost on him. I guess I should have picked a different way to express my gratitude, like telling him directly. Naw, that would be too emotional and uncomfortable. Let me stuff my feelings back down and get back to the advice givin' and book writin'.

I don't know how much you have interacted with the public, be it trying to order a meal at a restaurant, rebook a flight or even see a healthcare professional, but the bar for competence has never been lower. It has never been easier for someone to stand out for positive behavior. For example, my wife and I were at a well-known retail store to pick up a fireproof safe. We had ordered it online and were coming to pick it up, which involved going to the front of the store to have the people working at the front tell the people in the back to help us load it up. It was not complicated, but the staff working there were having a hard time with the concept of online order and pickup. Anyways, a 20-something female took charge of the situation, got our info, and barked the orders on the walkie-talkie to get our safe ready and that we'd need some help loading it.

As my wife and I drove to the back of the store, we both looked at each other and said, "I am not worried about that girl." Just her confidence, demeanor, and general ability to interact with the public showed us that she could tackle life's inevitable problems. We also vowed that it would be a bar to set for raising our kids. And you know how they could get there?

1) Show up on time.
2) Work hard.
3) Be easy to work with.

Beyond the world's problems and bleak employment prospects, parent naysayers like to discuss how dangerous and challenging raising kids is "these days." Which is not without danger nor without challenge. But kids have been poppin' out for thousands of years (depending on your religious persuasion). In peacetime. In wartime. In Miller Time.

In fact, there were even kids conceived and birthed during the Holocaust. You know, the thing that a lot of antisemitic Neo-Nazi types think was faked. It really happened, and there's a great book about it called *Born Survivors*. You should read it, and it will make almost any trial or tribulation you face here in the modern-day US of A feel pretty trivial.

On the other hand, I don't want to dismiss the very real concerns of being a dad. There are certainly risks with having kids. Big risks. Scary risks. Most of the anxiety and issues I see with dads are not *the* risks but in trying, in vain, to create a *zero-risk* environment for their kids. And take it from me, a Millennial from the "Nerf'ed" generation, who was brought up to try and be in a safety bubble as much as possible. The grim reality is: there is no such thing as zero risk.

I'll leave it to the pediatricians to give the specifics, but yes, in the first three months, your new baby is at their most vulnerable state. But as they grow, the bad news is they are going to get sick. I have many friends and family who have tried to keep themselves and their kid(s) in a bubble, avoiding family gatherings (not always a bad thing, in my opinion; Refer to "Silo of Sanity") and friendly get-togethers in a fruitless attempt to keep from getting sick.

It never works, and the only thing they end up avoiding is living a full life. Does this mean you should go have your kids lick doorknobs at public restrooms? Not on purpose, but if they are anything like my kids, they'll find a way. However, in trying to stay in a bubble, you are depriving yourselves and your kid(s) of a full life. Not to mention the chance to actually give their immune system a chance to flex its muscles, grow, and be useful at preventing illness someday.

What should you do? Take reasonable precautions: wash hands, don't go out if the kids are really sick, eat healthy, and sleep as much as possible for you and your kid(s). To put your mind at ease, the day we brought our first kid home from the hospital, we had a parade of friends and family come to the house, wash their hands, say "hi," and hold Jacob. Our second son was born in June 2020, during full-blown COVID. We still had family come over and say "hi" as long as they weren't sick. You can judge as much as you'd like, but you try telling my father-in-law he can't hold his grandson. Chuck wouldn't have any of it. And if I ever wanted to use his wood chipper again, it was in my best interest to let him hold Henry. Both sets of parents were there to greet us when we got home from the hospital with Henry, and it's a memory we'll cherish forever.

Ultimately, you have to do what you're comfortable with. And by you, I mean the baby's mom. Happy wife, happy life. Am I right?

As a result of some of the caution that is exercised with kids, one reservation I get from possible future dads is the worry that you'll screw them up. I want to end this chapter by putting your mind at ease and telling you not to worry about screwing them up. Because it's going to happen anyways. So, you may as well accept that it's not *if* you screw them up, but *how*. Someday, maybe they'll be upset you didn't hug them enough... or too much. Inevitably, as it was for me with my parents, hindsight is 20/20. I don't need to get into the myriad of things I have been trying to undo from my childhood, but in conversations with my friends, it sounds like it wasn't just my parents. I know they did the best they could with the resources that they had at the time. Most importantly, I have forgiven them, and hopefully, your kids will too. You'll have nothing to be ashamed of as long as you:

1) Show up on time.
2) Work hard.
3) Are easy to work with.

Chapter 4

What's in a Name?

Alright, so you've parsed out the pros and cons of kids, ignored the haters, and prepared for the event as much as physically and emotionally possible. Oh, and you did *it*. Maybe a lot. Maybe those swimmers of yours did their best Michael Phelps impression and found that egg on your first try. Whatever route you took, I hope it was enjoyable because you won't get that kind of free time to bone until your kids are out of high school. And by that time, you will be so old and broken that nothing will seem pleasurable anymore. Hurray, thanks for that, kids!

As you prepare to bring the little guy or gal home from the hospital, you have probably been gathering supplies for the baby. If you are like most new dads, you have probably gathered way too much. Don't feel bad! It's because you care, and boy, do we need more parents who care! But part of overbuying for your new baby may not have been consciously caring, but instead could have been fueled by targeted media ads telling you what "essentials" you will need. Another source of buying too much baby crap is the constantly bloated "suggested" baby shower lists generated by retail stores. Stores whose motivation isn't to provide the essentials, but to make as much money from anxious new parents as possible. There is also the chance for an earnest desire to avoid needing something and not having it on hand.

I can say from our personal experience, we ended up returning a lot of those baby shower gifts...unopened. When it comes down to the essentials of a new baby, they were (for us at least):

- Buttload of diapers (pun intended)
- Buttload of wipes (pun intended)
- Place for baby to sleep, be it a crib or a bassinet
- Stroller
- Swaddle blankets
- Few onesies (they outgrow these fast, and you'll do enough laundry to never touch many of the cute clothes from that bloated baby shower)
- Burp cloths
- Bottles/breast pump
- Car seat (don't forget to bring it to the hospital, or you don't get to take the baby home!)

Just those will be enough to keep the baby clothed, fed, and not covered in its own surprisingly not terrible-smelling baby poop. That's right, baby poop, at least from breast milk, doesn't smell that bad. Not that I recommend sniffing the stuff, but between the sleep deprivation, change of routine, and total loss of freedom, I'm sure you figured you could use a win. I will talk more about toys and travel later on in the book, but keep this in mind at all times with kids: simplicity wins.

Say My Name, Say My Name

Odds are that if you have figured out the gender, you have a name picked out. Or if you are bolder and actually patient like our neighbors and wait until the baby is born, you have a contender from each side of the aisle. Otherwise, if you are like our other neighbors, the name was an afterthought for a couple of days. In any case, this kid is going to have to go by something other than "Cut that out!" or "Stop hitting your brother!"

Now, I want to approach this subject gingerly, as in I am a white dude with some strawberry blond in my beard. Names can be a very cultural thing, and I want to acknowledge that. However, this brief section is speaking mostly to my fellow WASP-Y crowd, who have felt the need to create an "uncommon" name to make sure their kid feels unique, special, and loved. And probably made fun of.

My wife and I decided on a few pragmatic parameters when picking our names. You may agree, disagree, or try to cancel me on the internet. I am mentally prepared for that. But we were going off the basic assumption that:

A name does not make you special. Only *you* can make your name special.

As a result, our first parameter was simplicity and, in a word, boringness. Our kids got nice, unimaginative, boring names. We then had a set of three rules that would govern

53

our final choice:

1) Gender unambiguous
2) Simple to spell and pronounce
3) Something we could yell repeatedly and not grow tired of

Allow me to elaborate:

On point one, gender unambiguous; we just didn't want people to have to guess. There was an old Saturday Night Live sketch whose entire premise was based on the character "Pat," whose gender was ambiguous. The sketch's main driving comedic point was that the other characters were trying to figure out if Pat was a man or a woman. It was even made into a movie, "It's Pat." Neither the sketch nor the movie could be made today, in 2023. Based on the Rotten Tomatoes score of 0, that may be for the best on many fronts.

Regardless, you can call us old-fashioned, but we just wanted names that were clearly matching the genders of our boys and girl. Do what you want, but I know that my kids' names will never be made into something that scores so low on the "Tomato-Meter."

On point two, a lot of parents want to give their kids regular names with unique spelling, again, to help them feel special. I could go over the myriad of odd spellyngs of specific knames, but I want to proddect anyone who may feel bad about their own odd spellying. Instead, you probably have noticed that the last sentence had a lot of weirdly spelled but phonetically correct words. It made you think twice about what you were reading. Do you really want people thinking twice about your kid(s)?

I didn't thynk so.

On point three, my wife and I were on vacation in those sweet, sweet "before kids" times. In Kauai. It was glorious, kid-free, and relaxing. And we won't experience anything like that in a long time. But one day at the beach, a kid was playing in the ocean. And based on the mom's reaction, they were *not* following the rules. So, the mother called out to little *Zion*.

"Zion, come closer."

"Zion, we need more sunscreen."

"Zion, leave that shark alone."

Now, I have nothing *against* the name Zion, but my wife and I made a pact that day, that name would not be our kid's name. If there is anything kids do, it's behave in a way that requires you to get their attention, over and over and over again, and hearing that name on repeat was not something my wife and I would be willing to do. So, if NBA star, Zion Williamson, is reading this, I am sorry for offending you. Perhaps you can offer an olive branch of a treaty and send me some courtside seats?

Anyways, I can say five years after getting Jacob and three years after getting Henry, I have yet to grow tired of having to repeat their names. I mean, I am not tired of the names. If they would behave more and not require such regular repeating, I would take that. Because I am writing and editing this book as Amber is gestating/being born, I have yet to test-drive Rule Three. But I am confident that it will stand the test of time, and if I grow tired of repeating her name, I can just channel my grandfather and give her a nickname. My cousin Meredith was "Hook-A-Duke" and my niece Maddie was "Suzy." Neither has any context, but they are fun and provide an alternative for verbalizing discipline.

How exactly do you go about actually *choosing* a name? I have seen it done in many different ways. We have friends who went on an app and did a sort of "Tinder for names" where they linked their account, each picked names they wanted, and the app spit out the top rated for both. I have another friend who went down the route of one of their favorite musicians. We sort of went down the route of sports for our boys and music for our girl. Jacob was inspired by one of the greatest pitchers in Chicago Cubs history, at least for a couple of seasons, Jake Arrieta. Cassie heard a mom mention to her daughter, "Let's go get your brother Henry" at a Cubs game and thought that was a lovely name she didn't hear often. Henry also happens to be one the greatest (fictitious) Cubs pitchers in history: Henry Rowengartner from the classic film *Rookie of the Year*. If Henry had been a girl, her name would have been Audrey. No music or sports connection; my wife and I just liked the name. Our neighbors named their daughter Audrey, so we didn't wanna be all copycat-y, and we landed on Amber thanks to the song of the same name by the band 311. If you are wondering where Cory came from, I am apparently named after former baseball player Cory Snyder. My sister actually picked from Cory, Ryan, and Brian. Well done, sis! Although when I researched Cory Snyder, I discovered Cory was actually his middle name, and James was his first name. So from now on, I guess you can call me Jimmy Jenks if I really want to be true to the namesake. However you decide to pick a name is up to you, but perhaps, this has been inspiring. Or horrifying. I can't tell how you feel, but I can tell you that picking your kid's name could be a life-or-death decision.

Along those lines, let me lock you back into something less likely to be offensive, and much more critical to the safety of your kid(s). The name you give your kid could have dire consequences in the real world. I know this because of the following true story from a friend of mine:

My friend has a son whose middle name is "Bear," and that is what he goes by. I am not here to judge why you wouldn't make the middle name the first name if that is what you were going to call someone, but such was the situation. My friend and Bear were out on a trail hiking in the woods. It was a beautiful area with trees, fresh air, and, apparently, bears. Are you seeing where this is going?

Bear (the kid, not the animal) likes to run far out in front of his dad when hiking. I think any sort of initiative and leadership skills like this should be encouraged in normal circumstances. On this particular hike, Bear went so far that my friend lost sight of him over the crest of a hill. Not wanting his son to veer off into the wilderness, my friend then yelled loudly,

"Bear!"

He was able to get his son's attention, which was good. He also convinced a forest full of hikers that there was a bear nearby. Which sent them scurrying away, even though they didn't know where "away" was from the nonexistent bear. Anyways, I bring it up to show you how important choosing a name can be.

A name could cause confusion.

A name could cause chaos.

A name could cause someone to not heed the cries of "Bear" the next time there is a large mammal looking for a meal.

So, when it comes to a name: choose wisely.

Chapter 5

That's It?!

I wrongly assumed that when my first kid was born, some-thing magical would happen. Like on TV or in the mov-ies, when the clouds part, the music plays, and a sappy montage flashes through the main character's mind before they utter something totally profound. When we went into the hospital to have our first son, I thought I would have my magical movie moment.

As a Dad, that was not the case.

As a pharmacist who went into the profession to avoid fluids and holes, it was actually a little gross.

When our son was born, he was covered in what I assume is the medically accurate term "goop." He seemed pissed to have been roused from his quiet, cozy, comfy womb, and based on the noisy, stupid world he was entering, I think he was onto something. Once they wiped the goop off, they cut the umbilical cord. Leading up to the big day, many people had been asking me if I was going to cut the cord. I said I had already gotten rid of cable, and they then redirected me to the fact that cutting the umbilical cord was a dad's duty.

I was a bit concerned because even though I am a medical professional, I am not trained in surgical procedures. Cutting the umbilical cord seemed like an important duty, and if I messed that up, my kid, who had just met me, would already have a reason to resent me right out of the womb (not knowing that there would be plenty of other times for him to find reasons to resent me). Also, the thought of it really grossed me out.

Well, it turns out that the cutting of that cord is now a symbolic gesture, as they take a portion of the cord that has already been cut and have you cut it. However, I wanted no part of that either. It seemed silly and needless extra work, considering how much I was paying to have the baby be born.

I'm sorry, we got sidetracked by that hot umbilical cord talk. Where were we? Oh yeah, the kid covered in goop. Well, they used some sort of "magical medical towel" to wipe him off,[15] and the OB doctor handed him off to the neonatal doctor. At that point, I followed them to the "baby staging area," where my son got his vitals checked, his Hep B vaccine, and some eye drops. It would also be where he let us know what he thought of the absurd hidden costs of a hospital stay by peeing on the neonatal doctor.

My little man.

Finally, after they checked his vitals, pissed him off with

---

15   *It was just a hand towel, but based on the itemized hospital bill, that expensive piece of cotton should have had some magic in it.*

a vaccine, and topped off his wiper fluid, it was time for me to hold him.

Okay, here comes the magic movie moment I have been waiting for, I thought to myself. The doctor handed me Jake and said, "Congrats Dad."

Then, I held my son for the first time.

And nothing really happened.

I mean, it was cool and special, but if you have not been around a newborn much, they don't really *do* anything. I wasn't sure what I was expecting, maybe a high five, or a "thanks for plowing mom so I could be born." But he just kinda laid there in my arms.

Hmm, *I guess I'm a dad now.*

I was holding Jake while he was still fresh on April 12th, 2018. Having a baby did not solve my problem of what to do with both my hands in a picture.

At that point, after holding my goop-free, urine-liberated son, my wife had gotten out of recovery and was waiting to see and hold Jacob.

I brought him in and put him in Cassie's arms. He immediately started breastfeeding. It seemed he was much more excited to see her than he was to see me and for good reason. Thus began what I like to call "The Mom Show," and five years since it still has not stopped.

I'm Not Sure My Kids Love Me

I am not *bitter* about my kids' dependence on my wife. I would argue it is just part of biology. Newborns need to eat, they eat breast milk, and I cannot produce breast milk. Therefore, naturally, a new baby is drawn to Mom. There's also the part where they were joined at the placenta for nine months. Have you ever been joined at an organ to your kid? Then how can you expect to have any kind of a bond like that?! After a newborn comes into this world, they will be dependent on Mom for food, comfort, and generally, Mom has a more solid ability to "hush" the little baby.

So, what is a dad to do?

My non-expert advice is: everything else. I had such profound guilt that my wife was up every couple of hours to feed our son; there was *literally* nothing I could do to replace that. So I figured if my wife was feeding our son, I would feed my wife and, by default, be feeding my kid and thus, actually feel like I was contributing.

As a result, this meant a lot of cooking and cleaning, among other chores, and generally, "rah rahing" my wife through the challenging world of breastfeeding, lack of sleeping, and overall mom badassery. Maybe this seems untraditional, but I felt it was necessary to keep the house rolling along. Plus, I am not ashamed to admit I am a better cook than my wife. She's not a bad cook, but I have never seen someone with such a lack of feel for salt. Her idea of "salt to taste" is to imagine everything we cook needs to be "dolphin enjoyable." Anyways, it was not a terrible transition to taking the reins of these duties.

As my kids have grown, I thought that maybe the mom show would go on break while the writers prepared for the next season. That has not been the case. As a dad to a five-year-old, my kids *still* wake up in the middle of the night, either scared or covered in urine, and demand Mom. When my youngest was just two years old, I would go into his room to try and soothe him while he was crying, and he would say, "GO AWAY, DADDY. JUST MOMMA!"

In case you think I had forced some sort of abuse on them, I had not. They just *really* find comfort in their mom's arms. I had to learn to negotiate with terms like:

"I'll rub your back for a bit and then get mom."

"If you don't stop crying, I won't get mom."

"Do you know how much you are hurting my feelings right now?"

I can't guarantee your situation will be the same as mine, but I figured I could prepare you for what I could only assume is a worst-case scenario. On the other hand, there's a chance your kids won't feel quite an attachment to their mom, and will be more open to having you, um, lightly interact with them. But this is a dad advice book, and I want you to be prepared to take on the needed role of mother caregiver at the very least. Also, I don't want you to have the same level of surprise/disappointment in case your kids don't feel the need to show you love. I should have added that under *another* "reason to not have kids:" seeking the love and affection *from* them. There is no promise that this will happen.

On the other hand, there is also a chance that this is a "Mama's Boy" phenomenon. I have friends with little girls who are *super attached* to their dads. Since I am writing this before my daughter will have the chance to reject me, I am hopeful that the third time is a charm in the "kids overtly loving me" department.

And I don't want it to sound like my kids *don't* love me. They do. In fact, our second son even had a brief period of "dad attachment." It was really awesome. Then he quickly outgrew it. But even if your kids are drawn to mom for their comfort and seemingly every other need, they do *need* you. To take care of them however you can, to give them attention, and as we'll talk about next, to just exist with your *presence*. Because while my kids don't cry out for me in the middle of the night, my wife will say when I am *not* around, they often ask to make sure "Daddy knows" something cool they did, or to make sure "to tell Daddy to watch me when he gets home."

Unless, of course, she's just trying to help bolster my low dad self-esteem. At this point, I don't really care. I'll take whatever I can get.

Chapter 6

All It Takes is Being Present

A lot of newish dads wonder if they will be "enough" for their kids. Will they make "enough" money to support their family? Will they provide "enough" emotional support? Will they be "enough" for their kids to love them or at least tolerate them?

To make this happen, dads can sometimes go overboard working, trying to pry the feelings out of their kids, and smothering their kids with so much love that the kids will actually push away. I shared those feelings of needing to be enough. While more money is nice, it is important to be a loving and emotional pillar. There is just one trick to success as a father: be present.

I can't count how many times I have seen kids at the park, at home, or anywhere out just begging their dad for attention. And you may know where I am going with this if you have looked around at all in society. It is often the case that those dads have their faces buried in their phones, probably handling a very important fantasy football roster move. Or reading some news story that won't change anything. Or liking a meme.

And all that kid wants is to have their attention.

Many future and current dads (and moms, for that matter) think parenting needs to be a complicated, deeply thought-out process. That if we don't do everything in just the right order at just the right time, our kids will be deeply scarred for life. In order to try and crack that code, we are putting our noses in our laptops and phones, vigorously Googling[16] for all of the "right things" to do. Yet, while we spend that time searching on how to be a good parent, we don't realize how our kid(s) are standing there, waiting for us to give them our attention.

If you are ready for a dated '90s Pop Music reference, then here it comes: Isn't it Ironic? Alanis would be so proud of my having remembered her catchy tune, but she would be so disappointed in us as parents.

Following the above, I probably will start getting hordes of angry dads and moms contacting me because either some of you will be curious as to how the male mind approaches parenting or your husband has said, "Cory said to stop checking Instagram and that you're hurting our kid." Not to mention, you will perhaps want to tell me how essential your phone use is, and I will qualify all

---

16   Or Duck Duck Go-ing for you libertarians out there – Big Tech can pry our search history from our cold, dead hands.

and had multiple grandchildren.

As explained, I have 30 pictures. And proof that he was the most social person at his old folks' home.

Imagine if we had the recording power today back in the 1940s. If you think there is a lot of WWII content already, there would be no way to sort through all of the images and videos depicting our struggle against the Axis powers. Not to mention, as evidence of my grandfather's incredible and interesting life, I have a few dozen pictures. And you know what? It's enough.

On the other hand, you might be thinking, "Cory, that's a cherry-picked data point on a member of your family who clearly did not prioritize documenting their life. That's not fair. Stop making me feel bad for taking pictures of my kid."

Now remember, I did say I had another grandfather we could look toward for inspiration. Hold your horses. And hold your phone in a "non-picture-taking position" for a few seconds. Also, my grandfather was a hero, so don't insult his memory by insulting his proclivity for picture-taking. In all fairness to him, he was not mechanically or technologically inclined. Despite serving as an engineer in the Army, where he built bridges and disarmed Nazi land mines, he could never figure out a VCR, and I never saw him pick up a tool. I think that's a pretty incredible testament to either the Army's ability to train anyone for a job or the very low bar that was set as necessary in order to fight a global war on two fronts.

Speaking of the Army training people for a job, let me tell you about my other, handier, and more picture-taking grandfather. My dad's dad, henceforth known as Harry or Grandpa, was also an Army vet who spent his time in the service driving amphibious DUCKS and, by the looks of his old pictures, hanging out in Greenland. Grandpa could fix anything and would routinely dumpster-dive for old vacuums, washing machines, and anything that someone else had (wrongly) determined was no longer functional. He then fixed them and sold them by leaving them out on his front lawn or by posting them in the newspaper. Simpler times. And while it has nothing to do with taking pictures, I just wanted to brag about how badass Grandpa was.

Anyways, Grandpa was more of a photographer than Poppa. I think he had the same film-loaded camera (remember those?!) for 30 years. Unlike today's digital photography options, where the number of pictures you can take is nearly unlimited, as our oldest likes to prove when he snaps 100 pictures of the picture he colors, Grandpa had 25 chances with each roll of film.[19] Not to mention, that film did not come cheap, so he had to be judicious with his picture-takin.' And judicious he was because, despite decades of Kodak memories, 25 pictures at a time, when he and Grandma passed away, there were only five to ten physical photo albums in their house. For 182 years combined of life. That also included their wedding pictures and Grandpa's army pictures. In other

---

[19] I am pretty sure he was the last person in his small town of Boonville, New York, still using physical film. I remember in 2019 going to the Rite Aid with him and he went to the (mostly digital) photo counter, just dropped his roll of film down, pointed at the person working and at the film, and just walked away. They knew what Harry wanted. And Harry wanted his pictures taken care of so he could go buy scratchers tickets and the Boonville Herald.

words, the man knew how to pare down his albums before minimalism was a thing.

But you know what the cool part about those photo albums was? It was enough. Enough for four kids and seven grandkids to select memories to keep. And you know what? Aside from having his nose down, jackknife out on a scratcher while watching "The Wheel," and his photography proclivity, Grandpa was able to be pretty darn present with us.

So, Grandpa found a way to leave a nice assortment of memories for us kids. Yet in today's world, with an unlimited roll of digital film in each of our pockets, the documenting of life can get a bit out of hand. As a result, it can sometimes play tricks on our minds.

"AM I HONORING THIS MOMENT?!"

I remember a friend of ours who had their first kiddo about a month before ours yelling this, mostly in jest, as our two babies played cutely together as she felt the pull to take out her phone and snap a picture or video. It was a refreshingly honest and funny take on how the digital era parent feels the need to wrestle with being present while recording all of the adorable moments of our kids' lives.

What is a modern dad to do in such circumstances? Record too much and miss being in the moment, and at worst, ruining the moments of our kids' lives by recording it? Record too little and regret all of the times that will fade into the mists of history? At this point, I think we need to accept a simple truth:

It can't and shan't all be recorded.

There, relax. It is literally impossible to record everything awesome, hilarious, or embarrassing your kids do. Even if you did, good luck organizing what you've documented in such a way that you can easily access them. Of course, you could always raid your kid's/kids' college savings account for more Google Drive space if you really need to keep everything.

If it helps you relax, it may help if you realize that as much as you think you'll want everything, not everything needs to be recorded. My wife and I had a realization looking back on the number of pictures from our firstborn to our second. There was way more of everything related to Jake than to Henry. As a quick aside, if Henry is ever reading this, we are sorry there are fewer pictures of you, in which case we were probably more present with you than we were with Jake. Of course, you were too young to remember. And now you are a middle child, so we can add insult to injury. The good news is I think you have the temperament to handle it. And if not, we'll help pay for that therapy, buddy.

Pardon my digression to assuage the feelings of my middle child. It can be tough navigating the digital recording era of dadding. Therefore, my wife and I have developed some simple rules when it comes to taking pictures that I think may help you in your documentation journey:

- No pictures of landscapes: If there are no people in the picture, we are not taking it. A beautiful sunset over the beach is cool, and if I really want a picture of it, I can Google one. Live in the sunset with your family.

- When going to a landmark or a place where we would want a picture, we take one at the beginning and put the phone away: Think of any trip or vacation. How does it start? Super fun and awesome, full of anticipation! How does it end? Tired, cranky, and probably a little bloated. Get a picture at the start, put the phone away, and be with your family.

- Keep videos short: Have fun trying to share that five-minute file you just had to get waiting for Old Faithful to explode.

- Videos are horizontal: This is mostly for the Boomer Grandparents. If you are 45 or younger, you probably get this joke.

- If they've been here before and done it before, no pics/vids: Our boys love to wrestle. We have a couple awesome videos of what we call "Thor vs. Hulk" action. From now on, phones stay down, and we stay in the moment with them. Also, it's less evidence for CPS to take the kids away.

- We pare down the pics/vids the day they are taken: our digital memories can pile up fast, and they aren't always what we want to keep. Stay on top of it like weeding a garden.

- Dad makes year-end movies: A new spin on the "home movies," but with video editing software and an ample music library, I chunk up the year into 5 or 6 sections (none more than 10 minutes) and make movies with the photos and videos from the year. It's a fun way to relive your memories and is easier on the eyes than craning your neck looking at a phone.

You can take or leave these rules, but it has helped set boundaries from the annoying over-documenting and oversharing that goes on (I'll get more to oversharing in the social media portion of the book). Maybe our kids will appreciate having just enough pictures and videos of themselves from when they were young. But as I'll address in the future updated edition directed towards parents of teenagers, they probably won't.

Don't *Make* Memories...*Live* Them

It took 12 hours of driving, round trip. Two VRBOs. Two flights. And seven nights. It wasn't easy, but in the summer of 2022, my wife and I managed our four-year-old, (almost) two-year-old,[20] and my parents. We saw bison, played in rivers, and hiked to waterfalls. Old Faithful faithfully erupted, we hit an altitude so high that my kids got to see real snow for the first time, and my dad was satisfied that he had crossed off an item from his own Bucket List.

These were truly memories to last a lifetime, and as I discussed in the "documentation of life" section above, it made for a pretty awesome iMovie compilation. When we got back to Tucson, it was 110 degrees, our kids were hangry, and my wife and I were exhausted. But we had pulled it off, dammit.

As parents, we hope to create lasting memories for our kids. So, it was a perfect summation of how it goes with

---

20   *Travel hack: travel before they turn two and the plane ticket is free! Of course, you'll pay for it with a squirming toddler on your lap.*

kids when we asked our oldest what his favorite part of the trip was:

"Sonic."

After five states, thousands of miles, numerous toddler meltdowns and cave-ins for treats, his favorite memory of this Yellowstone (and Grand Teton!) trip was watching Sonic the Hedgehog on the iPad on the plane. I'll address my recommended use of tablets later, lest you should judge me right now. I bring this story up because a lot of advertising for travel, hotels, and experiences directed toward parents is meant to tug at your desire to create those *lifelong family memories.* And that's all well and good.

But you can't *make* the memories happen.

Whether you are taking your kids somewhere that was special to you as a kid, hoping they'll find the same joy (they won't) or somewhere new that promises an ultimate chance to make memories, your kids will make of it what they make of it. Have you ever seen those parents at the airport, amusement park or beach, yelling at the kids something along the lines of, "This is special! You need to appreciate how hard it was to get here! You will remember this for the rest of your life!"

Oh, they'll remember all right. Remember how much spittle was gathering on your lip as you yelled at them to MAKE MEMORIES.

Now, this doesn't mean not to try and have fun times with your kids. The advice is so that you let go of any perceived control you think you may have on the situation. My wife spent two years in Norway as a teenager due to her dad's service in the military. Norway sounds pretty awesome, right? Fjords. Snow. Um, universal healthcare? But she recalls being a snooty teenager who didn't appreciate how cool it was at the time. Because she was a snooty teen.

What it comes down to is doing your best to enjoy the moments with your kids and letting go of the memories you *try so hard to make* in order to embrace the memories you will make when you are able to be present.

Also, unless your parents have Yellowstone on their Bucket List, I don't recommend taking toddlers.

Chapter 7

If It Ain't Broke, It Will Be

D o you like some of the nicer things in life? If you do, there's no shame. We all have our things that light us up. Maybe it's collecting sneakers. Or perhaps you like nice cars. I was always a fan of sunglasses—Oakleys to be precise. These are our possessions. We worked hard to earn the money to have them, and you should enjoy them.

However, you can forget about any "thing" being sacred or safe anymore.

Your baby/babies, especially your toddler(s), won't care about the fact that those pair of Oakleys cost 300 dollars or that your car is brand new. They only know that things are shiny so they want to grab them. Also, they figure that taking their shoes off and dumping sand out in the car is more fun than dumping it outside. Most likely because they get to see how red your face gets as a result.

All of this is to say that the things you thought were yours aren't really yours anymore. So, you better get used to it. Therefore, I wanted to provide a few simple tricks to get you through the "break everything" phase of life, which, from what I hear from parents of teenagers, is a phase that never truly ends.

Firstly, get yourself some cheap sunglasses. As I alluded to earlier, I am a fan of Oakleys. Or at least I was, that is. Maybe it was because I grew up being a baseball player and saw that's what everyone else wore. Maybe it was because I got the hand-me-downs from my dad, who also foolishly liked expensive sunglasses despite being a public school teacher. But I liked what I liked.

Then, my kids came along. With the rush of "kids' stuff" to keep track of (I'll have more on limiting the amount of crap related to kids in chapter 9), the lack of time, and the curious hands that liked to grab anything shiny, having anything expensive sitting on my face, around the house, or in the car, became a dangerous and expensive proposition. As I said earlier, you can replace sunglasses with any number of expensive, easily breakable, and/or stainable items. Regardless of how much you say, "Don't touch; these are daddy's favorite sunglasses," your kids will only hear you say, "Daddy wants you to break these, along with his will and soul."

What should you do to combat their mission to destroy your personal property? Take some advice from the heavily bearded American Classic Rock Band ZZ Top,

"Get yourself some cheap sunglasses."

For you, this could literally mean sunglasses. But it could also mean any number of needlessly expensive things you used to purchase in "BK" (that's *before kids*) times, including shoes, shirts, jeans, baseball cards, and fine pottery. Why? Because your kids will find a way to break and/or lose them. When they do, and they will, you'll have no one else to blame but yourself. An added bonus of spending less on these easily breakable and/or losable items:

You can buy multiples. This can come in handy in a couple of ways. Firstly, when your kid breaks the item, you can just replace it with the extra you have. The other way is, or at least in our house, having a system of sunglasses: one pair in each car, one pair by the keys for when we go for a walk, and one really run-down pair for yard work. It will help you never go anywhere without them. Unless, of course, you are my wife and, therefore, *always* bring the car pair inside, totally negating the foolproof system I have devised.

So maybe, get yourself some cheap sunglasses even if you haven't had kids yet. Spouses are a great tune-up for the reality that will hit you.

Speaking of spouses, you will want to work together on your living space and make your house a *home*. I won't assume you are a homeowner; maybe you are a home renter. Just don't be a home-wrecker, amiright?! Because your kids will be more than happy to wreck the hell out of wherever you are living, staying, visiting, or squatting. Let's make one thing clear: this does not give you a license to live in total squalor. We keep it pretty tidy in our house, and as we'll discuss later, we don't let the mountains of kid crap overwhelm ours and our kids' senses. But if you think your walls, floors, and countertops are escaping unscathed from fatherhood, you are sorely mistaken.

We moved into our current house in 2019. It was a remodel and flip. The original plan for the previous owners was a "remodel and live in," but the owner, who also was a real estate agent, was about 6' 8," and his head almost hit the ceiling. He felt cramped and wanted to sell. Finally, a win for us short guys. It was a recent flip with the walls as blank slates, a nice off-white color, no holes from previous picture frames, and no scratches, dents, or dings. *Turnkey*, as they say in the real estate business.

About a month after moving in, we hosted a "housewarming/Jake's first birthday party." Having so many friends and family over, we got questions along the lines of "What color are you going to paint the walls" and "How are you going to decorate everywhere?" Having one kid about to be mobile and having been convinced to try for another kid, my wife and I realized the storm of kid chaos that was to come. So, our answer on painting and decorating was, "No new paint and very little of anything on the walls."

This has turned out to be a wise choice because those walls that are "yours" will no longer belong to you. It is your kids' world, paint canvas, and a place to test out their favorite color of markers. While you may think that "I'll just tell my kids *not* to color on the walls," remember how much toddlers will listen: not much.

It was only a matter of months for us before we saw our first green marker stain on the walls. My wife and I had made a conscious choice to accept what our walls were in for, so it was almost kind of cute. Almost. Since then, we have had:

- Nail polish on the tile floor (a pretty easy fix with nail polish remover)
- Our oldest marking days off a wall calendar and getting tiny little Sharpie dots on the wall
- A growth chart started by, again, our oldest by writing his and his brother's name in 6-inch letters

There is no point in decorating your walls at four feet or lower when your kids will just redecorate them for you like this DIY growth chart. Sadly, Jake's handwriting is better than anything I could have done anyways.

And that's only the stuff I have seen/had the will to deal with. My advice for you and your house is to keep it tidy, but accept that keeping a perfectly kept home is out of the question unless you want to spend all of your energy following/yelling at your kid(s) to not have any fun. And you don't want to be that kind of dad, do you?

Therefore, if you are fortunate to have the space for a playroom, make it a *play*room, Dad! Used furniture and nothing on the walls. Our kids' playroom has no pictures on the walls by design. Stuff is going to get thrown, and as a former baseball player, I actually want to encourage this kind of behavior. We have all kinds of soft balls my kids can go to town on working on that arm strength. I even put some painter's tape up in the shape of a square to get them trying to hit a target. My thought is rather than try and fight the instinct to throw in the house, create a fun place to do it with minimally damaging consequences (we have just accepted we will need to re-drywall the place multiple times).

We also got a used couch. Because your kids will want to make all the furniture theirs by climbing on them, jumping on them, and if they have siblings, pushing others off of them. In this room, you will never hear us say, "Don't climb on the furniture." That's their space. We also were gifted an old mattress we kept in there for a while. We called it our jumping mattress, and it was a place for them to get their "jumpies" out if they felt the need to jump on theirs or the urge to jump on our bed. They had a blast with it until it was destroyed by the physics equation of:

[mass x force x time = broken mattress].

And the best part about all of this? The price was *Free* dollars and 99 cents (we'll talk more about the "importance" of expensive toys later).

My favorite part of having this dedicated chaos/playroom was watching other parents freak out when their kid(s) started throwing anything that wasn't tied down against the walls and jumping over everything. We happily explained that we had given up on control, and this was the room for kids to "grip it and rip it." Some parents really appreciated the playroom. And some were never invited back to our house again.

I have mentioned a lot of physical possessions that will not really be yours, but I want to bring up one final thing that will never be yours again: time. That's it. Think you have time for that early morning workout? You better wake up even earlier. And even then, your kids will somehow wake up even earlier.

Think you have time to see a movie on Tuesday? Here I thought *I* am the comedian. Think you have time to chat with your wife before bed? Oh, they woke up at 5AM to steal your workout from you, and they'll be up until 9PM needing your attention today too.

I am not saying this to complain or to say how terrible being a parent is. I am just giving you the reality because you are on TKT now: that's, "Total Kid Time." And there is no Daylight Savings or rolling clocks back. However, there's just a lot of living on someone else's concept of time. No matter how often you say, "We need to be at school by 9. Let's go," the concept will never really sink in. Kids run on their own time, on their own schedules, and with no regard for how precious it is to you.

Plan accordingly because, like your sunglasses and the walls of your house: "your" time isn't really yours anymore once you have kids.

Chapter 8

Hills Worth Dying On

Having kids will change you. At least, if you are doing it right, there should be at least *some* changes. Like, putting your kid's needs (I didn't say wants!) before yours. Another change you are bound to encounter is getting weirdly overprotective about certain aspects of raising kids. In short: we all have our shit.

But if you make everything a priority to protect your kids from, or emphasize what they should be doing, then nothing will actually be a priority. My suggestion is to keep the "Hills Worth Dying On" to a short list of two to maybe three things that you think will have the biggest impact on the humans your kids will become. Because if you obsess over every little thing, you will drive yourself, and more importantly, everyone around you, crazy. Now, don't get me wrong, *helicopter* parents often attempt to control everything their kids touch, see, and eat with good intentions. But you know what the road to hell is paved with, right? Those devilish good intentions.[21]

Here are a few of the parenting hills my wife and I have lived and died on, and some other categories for your consideration. I'll even throw in some caveats about when we broke our own rules! Hurray hypocrisy!

The Movie Marathon

I wasn't sure if talking about food or screens would be the most divisive issue of this book and thereby lead to the most negative reviews of my book. So, I flipped a coin, and we're going with screens, baby!

Quick! Give me a list of all the reasons your kid(s) *needs* to be interacting with screens on phones, tablets, and TVs!

I'm waiting.

Still waiting.

Since you are reading this book long after I am typing these words, I should probably get going with my points, as I will never actually be able to read your answers. Unless you email them to me or post them in a scathing review.

I'll give you my list of the reasons kids need to be in front of screens, and we can compare notes:

Wow, hope it didn't take you too long to read that. In case you haven't figured it out, my wife and I are quite protective when it comes to our kids sitting in front of anything that glows and talks to them. Yes, that means

---

21   *Typing "devilish" reminds me that we have not made deviled eggs in our house in some time. What a wasted opportunity. Of course, as I type this in 2023, the price of a dozen eggs is roughly a car payment, so maybe that's why we've backed off the deviled egg construction.*

season had started, and my oldest asked me if "we could watch some baseball." Hell yes, son. Hell yes. While sports are mostly just an excuse to run commercials, I already touched on what I am teaching my kids about commercials. With an attitude like that, it's game on when the game's on.

- ☑ Getting something done: It could be dinner, it could be folding laundry, or it could be packing up for the park. Sometimes, you need your kids zonked out so you can actually get something done.

And that's about it. An argument I have heard is, "If I don't introduce screens to my kids, how will they ever understand technology?!" I assure you, these products are made to be easy to learn for any skill level. Heck, my dad is on Twitter. Your kids will be just fine.

Food for Thought

My wife and I both work in healthcare. She is a nurse practitioner, and I am a pharmacist. We deal with the consequences of poor lifestyle and nutrition all damn day. Every day. So, when we make the food our kids eat a hill to die on, it's because we have seen the time machine into our kids' future if we don't at least try and set them up on a path to dietary success. One argument I actually get from my patients when they eat junk food is that they have to keep it in the house "because they have kids." I'll remind you again about what I said in Chapter 20, but (THAT) you are the adult of your household. With that being said, my wife's and my crazy approach is:[23]

- **Nothing sweet before one year old**: That's right, we didn't even give our kids fruit until they were one. Feel free to gasp or call CPS. We don't really care. We didn't need our kids getting hooked on sweetness before they could appreciate it.

- **Only dark chocolate of at least 80% and not until two years old**: Can you believe our one-year-old didn't get a cake to smash and eat it for his birthday? Again, our food proclivities are being formed in those young years. If you think this is mean, please remind me of the best piece of pie you had at two years old. Can't remember? How about three? Four? I rest my case.

- **Piggybacking off the last one, no added sugar until about between the ages of three and four years old**: Our son's first real cookie was when he was three and a half years old, and it came from a neighbor and her three-and-a-half-year-old daughter. This is the rule that makes grandparents cringe. But hey, we said we picked a couple of hills to die on. Food was one. For as much resistance as our family gave us (our friends were pretty cool...to our face, at least), our sons are a couple of high-growth chart muscly studs. When they have a sweet, they usually eat it slowly, take a couple

---

23   *Whenever we go to a party or someone else's house and bring our own food, or our kids' food, we acknowledge we are weirdos. No point in pretending. But you know what normal is in America? Overweight and unhealthy. Dare to be weird, too.*

bites, and don't finish it. It may just qualify as a superpower.

- **Limited processed grains and no juice or crummy oils**: "Your kids don't eat bread. Or crackers. Or chips. What do they eat?!" The next point will explain what they do eat, but yes, for the most part, our kids don't eat grains. They don't get juice because I feel it is a totally unnecessary part of the diet and has just as much sugar in it as soda does. And crummy oils like soybean, canola, and anything else that is an oil, but is not naturally oily, are a catch-all for things that are generally not great for kids or your health. The great thing about the oil rule is it keeps out most processed junk food. Now, have we eased up as our kid has gotten older? Yes. And we are under no illusion that they will grow up and not eat garbage food. But it won't be from us. And hopefully, they will learn that when they eat garbage food, they will feel like garbage.

- **Protein with each meal**: Kids are growing, and that includes their bones, muscles, and connective tissue. Thus, our kids get protein each time they eat. For example, hamburger, deli meat, salami, and in a pinch, hot dogs (we buy the "Best of the Worst" when it comes to processed meats, but still think it's closer to real food than crackers and juice). Funny hot dog story real quick: my wife was going to a friend's house with the kids and brought a couple of cooked hot dogs (they were actually all beef polish sausage, but our kids don't know the difference) in her fanny pack in case they got hungry. The kids started acting like a-holes, which is code for: they needed to eat. So, my wife pulled out her "pocket dogs," fed the kids, and made quite an impression with the other moms. Before you judge us too much, they will get fruit, and yes, even some "treat foods." But it ain't before they get the essentials of what they need.

I have people close to me who refuse to eat leftover food. I am not sure if it's a sanitation thing, a boredom thing, or an "I'm above it" thing, but I will never understand that approach. Actually, let that be the first random lesson of this chapter! Get used to leftovers, Dad. It can be a challenge to have any meal freshly made (or freshly picked up/delivered via GrubHub), and when you add kids to the mix, there is even less time. The less you have to spend time cooking, the better. Leftovers are a huge part of our lifestyle, which, given how much my kids eat, I am frankly quite shocked. Nonetheless, we are in this thing for max results with minimal effort. Fire up the crockpot, make some big ass batches of whatever your specialty is, and dine like, well, kings never really had a hand in raising their own kids as far as I know, but you'll dine for several days in a row. So there's something! Check out the appendix for a few of my go-to multi-day recipes.

On a somewhat related topic, here's a phrase we have in our house: ABS— *Always Bring Snacks*. As crushing as our childhood and adult obesity rates are, kids are growing. Provided you are funneling them closer to the "more real

is tasked with a snack for each game/practice. This is in a pretty well-educated and compensated neighborhood, and our coach emphasized the need to bring "healthy snacks." One night after practice, we counted the grams of sugar in the "snack bag" to be over 70 for a snack right before they were supposed to go to bed at night. Multiply this well-intentioned sugar-ing across three to four meals a day, and it is no wonder our kids are in such miserable physical and emotional shape these days. I'll get off my soapbox and off this hill I am dying pretty hard on right now. In the back of the book, I have some dad resources, including a couple of excellent books on nutrition that hint towards our psycho approach to eating, as well as some slick recipes!

In case you were wondering, though, our boys have had cake. And ice cream. And cookies. And pizza.

Just not at the same time. I am not a monster.

But we have adjusted as the kids have gotten older. We are not over here trying to give them an eating disorder, but we have gotten a touch more lenient with what we call "sometimes foods." At pre-school, there is a treat sometimes, and we don't need our kid being the only weirdo never getting a doughnut. That will only lead to a Krispy Kreme rebellion in their teens. For special occasions, they get their special "sometimes food" treat. But we also bring our own Jenks-Approved treats to parties and gatherings when the sugar train has been rolling too hard through town. This is 85% dark chocolate, some sort of protein bar that is a little sweet, or we (by we, I mean my wife) will make some lower sugar versions of baked goods.

There is a balance to be struck, but I think the current societal balance is too far on the "they're kids; they need to have treats to have a good childhood." I'd argue we have gotten a little too far towards that side, and we are trying to foster the "our kids are still happily eating a bunch of protein and have fruit as a treat." But hey, this is our hill we want to die on.

Peer Pressure Starts Early

We are fortunate that, thus far, most of the kids with whom our kids have interacted and become friends have been awesome. More importantly, their *parents* are awesome. Alas, keeping our kids from certain friends has not been something we have had to deal with, but is something we have heard of others handling. I am sure in the teenage edition of this book, this section will be much more robust. But for now, keep an eye and ear out for odd or inappropriate stuff your kid says because, most likely, they heard it from a friend. If you need to keep your kids away, don't feel bad. Control this while you can. Because what we as a society think of as "normal" and "OKAY" for kids to consume is often wrong.

I have to admit, these are just the hills we have come across and died upon. The freeing thing is it takes all of the other mental bandwidth you could be worrying about and frees you from worry. We know people that insist their kids bathe every night. Not us. Don't mess up the house? Our house was made for messing up. Always look presentable? Our oldest son went to school with a hole in the bottom of his pants yesterday because we didn't feel like fighting.

The thing is, if one of these, or something else, *is* a hill you want to die on, don't feel bad! Having kids make irrational beings of us all. I am sure I will look back on some of the stuff I worried about and wonder what I was thinking...and the stuff I missed out on worrying about too. As I said, don't feel bad. As long as you acknowledge it's not always rational to other dads, like having hot dogs in your fanny pack. Or wearing a fanny pack.

Get the Message?

There are a few more small hills my wife and I will die on. We just don't accept, at face value, a lot of what is considered to be suggested reading for our kids. I will expand upon that shortly. But I'd like to aim at a couple of the stalwarts of childhood reading that have had it far too easy for far too long.

Pete the Cat

Do you want a series of stories teaching your kids how "awesome," "cool," and "groovy" it is to be mediocre? Well, then, maybe you shouldn't avoid this book and TV series. Unfortunately for us, Jake got into *Pete the Cat* before we realized what a horrible message he sends. In one story, Pete plays baseball. Okay, I like baseball. I was ready to get on board. Then, Pete strikes out, misses a ball in the outfield, and gets thrown out, probably at third base with less than two outs. Does the story say how Pete realized he hadn't practiced enough or that he needed to focus more while in the field? Nope. It was simply, "It's cool that he sucks and drags his team down."

When my wife and I read these stories, we editorialize significantly and add things like, "And Pete realized he didn't work hard enough and was going to practice more." You know, things you would want your kid to learn to do. Our kids really listen to the stories we read to them, so it's important to pick ones with messages you want them to follow. I was so hell-bent on ridding our house of *Pete the Cat* that Jake had a Pete stuffy he had loved, then forgotten about. So, on one of our "Minimalist House Cleanses," we gave Pete away. Unfortunately for us, Jake has an incredible memory, so when he asked about Pete, we had to fess up and say that it was our fault for getting rid of Pete, we were sorry, and we got him a new one. He never threw a fit or cried, but was earnestly sad about Pete being gone. My wife and I felt terrible and guilty and said we'd get him a new Pete.

He was very happy and excited for about a week. I am sure you are shocked to know that his new Pete sits at the bottom of the stuffy bin to this day. Groovy.

Curious George

If I haven't lost you yet, this one might seal it. Who doesn't love Curious George?! He's a cute monkey that's always getting into mischief. I'll get back to that, but first, have you ever read the first-ever *Curious George*? Because if you haven't, this entire series was spawned when George was essentially stolen from his happy jungle habitat by that poaching prick, *The Man with the Yellow Hat*. For all of the things PETA needlessly whines about, I haven't heard a peep from them about this fictional travesty.

But the reality is that George is here to stay, interacting with humans and sending poisonous messages to our kids. If you haven't read a lot about George, the premise of every story is basically this: The Man leaves George alone despite a history of disobedience. George ignores The Man's plea to stay out of trouble; George gets *in trouble,* causing widespread mischief, then George fixes his own mess.

And then, George is celebrated.

Oh, hurray for George!

What an awful message to kids: you can ignore rules and disrupt everyone else's day and plans, but it's okay if you fix the mess you made after misbehaving in the first place and will not only be accepted for it, but also celebrated for it. Don't think it's a terrible message? Imagine you told your kid to not play with a lighter, but they did play with a lighter and started a fire, but then put that fire out. Would you celebrate them? Or would you ground them? Maybe put them in time-out? At best, perhaps praise them for not totally burning your house down? But they would certainly not be the Hero of the Day.

I'll spare more commentary, but despite what parenting consensus deems as "normal" for kids, I think you and your kid's lives will be better by avoiding these options. Did I miss more? I am sure, but start with these, and be relentless in your shutting down of these mind-dumbing media options.

While your kid(s) between the ages of 0-five years are unlikely to be able to read, understand, or appreciate many of the adult books (like this one!), at some point, they will develop the trifecta of literacy, independence, and curiosity to do so. On the subject of reading, here is something that we have started in our house to help fend off the dumb literature available to melt malleable young minds: every time I read a book that leaves me asking, "Why the hell didn't someone teach me this when I was younger?!" I put it on our "Jenks Kid Reading List" for a future day. I also throw in some podcasts, blog posts, and videos that I think have valuable lessons. Most likely, your kids won't listen to you in the future, so why not let some of the smartest people in history teach them instead? Start cultivating that list today, and if you have a boy, why don't you put this book right at the top for their possible future Dadding experiences? They'll at least know who taught their dad some of the things that screwed them up.

Chapter 9

Too Much CRAP

H aving a kid, or in my case, kids, can add a lot of chaos to your life. And if you think there is a magic point at which the chaos starts reversing, you are probably reading this before having kids or have hired the rearing of your kids to an excellent nanny or au pair. Kudos to you, Dad; you are probably crushing it in your work and personal life since you have the money to farm out the rearing of your kids and thus, the time and sanity that is *not* spent cleaning up after your little monster(s).

But for those of us in the real world of hands-on kid-raising, the chaos remains. How can we manage it? Well, we can't stop it, but we can hope to contain it. And by it, I mean the amount of needless crap in, on, and around our houses in relation to our kids.

The Fat Cats in advertising and at "Big Kid" will have you thinking that if you are not equipped with every toy, device, and tool to raise your kids the right way, then you are failing as a parent, husband, and human being. The good news is that most of what they say is mostly junk, much like the crap they are selling. The bad news is that it can be hard to get out of the hedonic cycle of buying stuff, accumulating stuff, and trying to store stuff, thereby eventually being crushed (in a physical and metaphorical sense) by stuff.

For full disclosure, my wife and I found the Minimalism movement in the late 20-teens, and while we are not quite on the extreme end of owning almost nothing and liking it, we have found that eliminating garbage from our lives that we didn't enjoy really helps us focus on the most important things. Like our kids. Remember, your kids *are* important. Anyways, if a true "Minimalist" walked through our house, they would probably vomit in horror. An Instant Pot AND an Air Fryer?! More than one pair of shoes?! A room just for our kids to play in?!

Fortunately for us, the Minimalist police is not a real thing. But here are a few broad strokes to help keep your house in order as your kids bring their own disorder.

First things first: stop buying cheap shitty shit. Let me relate a slightly embarrassing story about my parents (sorry, love you, Mom and Dad!) to bring home the point of how often we can miss the actual point.

Climate Action Now

The big green sign signifying "Climate Action Now" sat in front of my parents' house as a signal of how virtuous they are. How much they care about the Earth. As far as people of the Boomer age go, it was refreshing to see

choose when it comes to raising my kids. If so, I'm sorry, but you've already read this far, so let's see how I can upset your sensibilities even more!

If you can't tell, my wife and I make a real effort to not overdo it when it comes to toys, especially cheap plastic crap that breaks right after you (or your parents) buy it for them. As much as it may seem like we are jerks, our kids do at least seem genuinely happy with what they have to play with and their overall lives. Of course, the final edition of this book that I'll come out with in 25 years dealing with your kids, their issues with you, and the best way to find a therapist will hopefully be helpful. Anyways, here are a few more suggestions on the toy storm that can develop with young kids.

Keep it simple: We have family and friends politely and good-heartedly ask what our kids want for their birthdays, holidays, and random days. We first try to get them not to buy our kids anything. When that doesn't work, we suggest a small donation to their 529 account. When that doesn't work, we have a few guidelines we request:

1. Nothing with batteries
2. Nothing that needs to be charged
3. Nothing with an insane number of small parts (that's more for our sanity)
4. Try to make it a consumable or an experience

By avoiding anything with batteries/charging, you will have freed up a large portion of your time paying for, charging, changing batteries, and listening to talking toys and annoying sounds ruining your life. For thousands of years, kids were somehow raised in a battery-free world where their toys didn't talk to them or light up. Yet somehow, our species was able to survive.

For example, a regular toy car is fine. A talking "Mater" from the movie *Cars* is totally unnecessary. I can almost guarantee the difference maker in your toddler's life will not be whether or not their toy car has Larry the Cable guy repeatedly telling them to "Git-R-Done!" It is very unlikely that years later, in their valedictorian speech, or while defending their PhD, that they will mention how the turning point in their life was when their car spoke to them and reminded them how important it was to "Git-R-Done" and that's how they had the fortitude to press through the adversity.

So, no batteries, no noise, and more sanity for you.

And speaking of sanity, unless we are talking Legos, Magnet Tiles, or Lincoln Logs, then games and activities with more than four parts should be banned from toy aisles. These "can only be one thing" toys like a science kit or intricate board game are a pain in the ass to clean up and are inevitably rendered useless when one piece goes missing behind the couch, under a rug, or on the floor of your car.

Speaking of having toys all over your own house or inside of your car, have you been to someone's house with kids who have piles, piles, and piles of toys? I find it overwhelming, and despite how much kids say they love having tons of toys, I think it overwhelms them, too. I don't say this as a judgment to the parents. Kids can be unruly. They whine. They demand. And society has set up an expectation of "more is better," not to mention the incessant commercials we are bombarded with on TV and Online.

So, keeping the toys limited takes active work. But you have read this far, so I know you are up for the challenge.

One of the approaches we have used, and by used, I mean stolen from other parents, is the idea of toy rotation. In an effort to keep it fresh and keep our floors from being a minefield of kids' playthings, we have a limited number of toys out at any given time. Every few weeks or so, we take some of the toys that the kids haven't used, put them away in a closet, and put some other toys out. It's like they are getting a new toy from the store. Gosh, kids are gullible; use that to your advantage!

This is our toy room. Offensively overcrowded to hardcore minimalists, and criminally "under-toyed" to those who think kids should have everything. I don't really care one way or the other because it's no more than five minutes to tidy this room up, even at its most chaotic, and our kids seem perfectly happy with the array of crap we have for them to play with. We get them to clean up by starting to do it ourselves and letting them know that our family is a team and we work together to clean up. It works amazingly well, and after a while, the kids start cleaning up themselves without prompting.

By doing this, we keep our toys limited and our space as neat as much as we can reasonably hope for with toddlers. I have no studies to back this up, but I am convinced that the kids are calmer and happier with a smaller number of choices to play with. Not to harp on our "no batteries rule," but they typically go back to the same few things: Legos and Magnet Tiles to build, balls and bats to play with, a few toy cars, and drawing/creating stuff with an assortment of drawing tools. As you can see, while our toy assortment may make a minimalist sick to their stomach, it certainly doesn't have the "room creep" we have seen at other houses.

We also like to keep things limited in our house. Like, we limit the amount of dumb content our kids watch that will wash their brains out and empty our wallets. Tops on our list: *Paw Patrol*. My first exposure to *Paw Patrol* was at a friend's kid's birthday party. It was just after Jake was born, and it was at a park outside. Okay, I can get down with the outside fun. And it was totally *Paw Patrol* themed. "Interesting" was the thought I had when I first heard about it.

Then I saw everything *Paw Patrol* themed, from the plates and cups to the cake and the kid's entire wardrobe. I did some intel, briefly watching a clip or two and reading a couple of their books.

It is a big ball of dumb. There are no real lessons. No real consequences. But what there is, is a never-ending assortment of *Paw Patrol* crap available for purchase that your kid will demand. There is literally nothing redeeming about this show, and I am not ashamed to say when Jake was gifted a *Paw Patrol* book, it got "lost."

He'll thank me later. Or hate me.

Aside from avoiding dumb shows, something else we have used with surprising success is as our oldest has become more sentient, we have discussed that other kids aren't as fortunate to have such a wide array of toys that collect dust and occasionally get used. So, it is a kind gesture to give some away from time to time. We really press this home when we know a new wave of crap is coming—like before birthdays and during the holiday season. This way, we get out in front of the inevitable tidal wave of toys. What has been cool is seeing our kid not only agree with us, but also start doing it on his own sometimes. There's a lot of time for him to get off the path of kindness, but it almost feels like we are possibly on the path of raising a decent human. Stay tuned for the next edition.

Be Lenient With...

Sorry again, nerds!

Much like my TV/Screens caveat, I am much more lenient with my rules when it comes to sports gear and outdoor equipment like shovels, wheelbarrows, and hula hoops. Part of me hopes they foster a love of the sport. But mostly, it's fostering their "love of doing Daddy's outside chores."

My wife and I had a goal when we bought our current house: to create a space for our kids to be outside as much as possible. I am not saying I never played a video game (or hours of Goldeneye, Mario Kart, and Tiger Woods

Golf), but some of my fondest memories and the best parts of my childhood were spent outside: riding bikes, playing baseball, and building forts.

I could keep listing outdoor activities, but I don't want to insult your intelligence. When shopping for our "forever home" in 2019, we had a choice of a newer, bigger house with a tiny yard or an older house that was smaller, but with a big ass yard. We went *big-ass-yard.*

It sounds like an old cliché to say that "kids these days spend too much time inside." But I think kids these days spend too much time inside. They'll have plenty of time to sit on their asses and stare at computer screens whenever they get whatever soul-sucking white-collar job awaits them, should they go down the college pipeline.

For now, let them play! We want our kids to be as comfortable outside and as athletic as possible. And, judging by the genetic lot they received, it's going to take a lot of work to get them athletic. When it comes to sports and outside toys, we are more apt to give in when our kids ask for something. Balls, bats, gloves, cleats, nets, bikes, scooters. If it gets our kids outside, then we are all in.

On the other hand, we are not climate-hating monsters. We spend a lot of time at *Play it Again Sports*, getting repurposed sports gear at a repurposed price. Getting kids outside doesn't need to break the bank, but as far as toy return on investment goes, we have seen much more from their sports gear than the RC car their grandparents gave them for Christmas. Anyone can push a button to make a car go, but to see the joy in our kids' faces when they have figured out how to hit a golf ball far, roller skate, or dig their own garden, as my oldest son is currently doing, is a truly awesome parenting moment.

Therefore, if you are going to splurge on anything, get them a few racquets, balls, and gloves and see what they can come up with. It is not only awesome to see their physical skills improve, but also amazing to see how they develop creativity by coming up with their own games.

I'll end the sports section with a recent anecdote. My son randomly asked to play racquetball, so I let him borrow an old racquet of mine. He loved hitting the ball around the house and wanted some balls of his own (wait 'til puberty, son), and his own new racquet. I said that I'd give him the racquet "for free," and he was elated until he also wanted a new grip on it. So off to *Play it Again*, where he bought his own balls with his own money (a proud parenting moment), and I got him a new grip.

While there, he saw a shiny orange t-ball bat, and with t-ball starting in just a few weeks, he asked if we could get it. He already had a t-ball bat, but it was a few inches too big because last year, Dad got a little overly excited at the prospect of his son playing t-ball and bought the only bat at the Big 5, even if it was a little large. Owning up to my mistake, I said we could come back with Mom and his little brother to get it later, which we did. While there, little brother wanted a helmet even though he was too young for t-ball. But seeing how hard Jake swung the stick, we figured some head protection would be good. We got Henry a used helmet while Jake got his shiny orange bat.

The next day, they wanted to go to the park to use their new goodies. We met my dad, with whom Jake wanted to play racquetball, and they did, which got my dad and Jake super excited. Then we went and tried out the new bat while Henry wore his helmet. As often happens with four-year-olds and baseball, Jake missed a few pitches in a row (a chip off the old block he is!). He finally connected and ran around the bases at the park while his brother cheered him on. But the unexpected part was the "crowd" that had gathered and started cheering as a group of high schoolers were hanging out playing soccer in the outfield. So, my son got to run around the bases for his "home run" while the crowd cheered him on.

Dude was pumped. Almost as much as I was.

When we left, one of the kids called out, "They're going D1 (Division One)!" I replied, "I hope they go in round 1; that's where the money's at!"

I tell this to show you why we invest in outdoor gear. I can also tell you that our kids have never been this excited or proud after watching three hours of *Octonauts*, or when playing with the talking electronic "Police Robot" they once got for Christmas.

While sports may not be your or your kid's thing, getting their (and your) ass(es) outside is probably one of the best things for them. And if sports are not your jam, you can get outside by digging in the dirt, going for walks, drawing with chalk, riding bikes and scooters, climbing trees, painting rocks, watching bugs, or playing at the park. Our kids like to hammer chalk and turn it into a powder, play with bubble bath soap in their water table, and dig for dinosaur bones. Just give them some space, free reign to be messy, and they will find some creative ideas. And while your kid is

Chapter 10

Invest in Good Underwear

Having some nice pairs of undies, boxers, briefs, or boxer/briefs really has nothing to do with being a good dad. But dammit, you deserve it. And you should be comfortable when your kids wake you up at all hours, and underwear is all you're wearing. So, get yourself some nice underwear. Your nether regions will thank me later.

Chapter 11

Take Off!

My boss was recently talking about his trip across the pond (from here in the US) to Scotland and England with his wife. How they had a 17-hour delay in getting there. And how, once there, they enjoyed eating at Michelin-rated restaurants. I was amazed by his travels. And totally related to his dining experience at highly-rated restaurants by explaining that I helped finish the uneaten end of my kid's hot dog the other day. He could not relate as he still has his "freedom." I mean that he doesn't have kids...yet. And if I keep sharing such fun parenting nuggets, he may never have them.

I am a parent; you are, too (or will be soon). Before we had kids, my wife and I did a lot of traveling around these great United States. In fact, in 2016, we did a "30 for 30" year, doing 30 trips and activities to honor the fact we were turning 30. In addition to providing insight on how old I am, it was an awesome year of memorable travel we made sure to savor because we knew kids were on the horizon.

On the other hand, if you love traveling and vacationing, having kids doesn't mean you don't get to travel again. It just means it's going to be different. And unless you are one of those Instagram freak families that live in an RV or show off their "jet-setting with kids" ways, you are going to need some simple, real-world tips for getting around with kids. The good news is my wife and I have continued to fly the friendly skies and hit the road even as our family has grown. I want to share some simple tips and tricks that have made our travel less painful.

Hit the Road Early

When Jake was four months old, we set off on a cross-country flight to upstate New York...with a pit stop in Pittsburgh. I know, I should have been a travel agent and not a pharmacist/comedian/writer. I can surely pick the hot spots. So why stop in *that* hot summer vacation destination? It wasn't a love of perogies; it was a quest to hit up every Major League Baseball ballpark. We were young, dumb, and ambitious. And it actually turned out to be a great time to travel with kids.

There are several advantages to traveling with an infant. Firstly, they fly free! Under two and in a lap means you don't have to shell out any extra money. Just your sanity. Joking aside, we went to Yellowstone in 2022, and the timing of the trip was based mostly on when Henry was going to turn two. And so it was; we went in early June, a week before his birthday. While it was hard having a huge, almost two-year-old on our laps, we saved several

- 🛁 Baby wipes/paper towels: Your kids are going to touch everything, and if you are changing diapers, too, this is another item you don't want to run short on.

- 🍿 Snacks: Airport food is tempting. I am sure it was probably engineered to be a coping mechanism for tired, frustrated parents strung-out on no sleep. It's also incredibly expensive and mostly terrible for your kids and you. You need to fuel up to be on top of your game. Also, if you feed your kids sugary trash, they'll probably behave accordingly. Also, *Sugary Trash* sounds like a great punk band name. This won't help you travel, but it will help you if you play the bass guitar.

- 🪑 Car Seat: If you are driving, this is obvious. If flying, I recommend checking it in if you aren't strapping your kid in. The airlines actually won't charge you for it. How generous of them! And if you get a good cover/case for it, you can sneak extra clothes/diapers into it, and you just treat it like a normal piece of luggage. Take that, ya greedy airlines! Plus, when your flight is delayed, you won't have to carry that AND your snot-nosed kid in a desperate attempt to make your connection.

- 🦆 Toys: Here is where most parents slip up, bringing an army of toys and only a squad of essentials like diapers, clothes, and snacks. You need not bring the entire library of books, nor the whole garage of Matchbox Cars. What you bring

133

will be kid dependent, but we find four to five toys are enough to get the job done. If your kid is old enough, a coloring book and some crayons could entertain them for hours. Or lead to a panicked clean-up of the window shade. But don't bring too many toys because....

- ☐Tablet: Or, as my wife and I call it, our "Break open in case of need of sanity" option. We make every effort to go as analog as long as possible, but we all have a breaking point. If you have been judicious and don't let them use screens all the time, it will be an effective, fun treat for them. A couple of tips: make sure whatever movie/shows you want them to see are pre-downloaded. You can only count on airport Wi-Fi to do one thing: let you down. Also, get some kid-friendly noise-canceling headphones, so you can talk all the shit about your kids that you want without them being scarred.

- 👮 TSA *PreCheck®*: Getting to keep everyone's shoes, jackets, and electronics stowed and worn where they are can save precious minutes and stress getting through the airport. It is hard enough getting kids, car seats, and all the other kid-related accouterments through the airport, make life easier, and drop the $80 for *PreCheck®*.

- 🧴 Water bottles on flights: Beware that the change in cabin pressure will create a fun geyser once opened at altitude. Well, it's fun for your kids to watch, but less fun for the unfortunate stranger who gets doused with a stream of water. Make sure to twist it open to first relieve the pressure. Or don't and get treated to a water show at 35,000 feet.

- ⚕️First Aid Kits: You are an adult, and should possess them, especially as a parent. Get one for each vehicle when traveling, and while you are at it, at least one extra-large one for your house. Your kids are going to hurt themselves, and possibly... hurt you, too. You can be prepared, or you can be the family known to be covered in blood. Your call.

Make it Fun, or Just Make It

Is traveling stressful? It sure can be.

Does adding kids ratchet up the stress? Undoubtedly.

Can the experience still be fun? Sure. If you block out all of the other pains of traveling (mostly kidding).

On the last two points above, regarding how to entertain your kids, my wife is the best at turning a possible turbulent traveling situation into a fun adventure. For our trip to Yellowstone, she got each boy a little toy/treat that they got at different trip intervals. Stickers for getting through airport security. A slap bracelet for getting on the plane. A coloring book once we were airborne. The kids loved it, and it kept them in their "variable reward dopamine hit" mode while entertained with their dangled carrots for good behavior. We made it almost all the way through our first flight without busting out the tablet.

On the return trip, we were too exhausted to care. They got to watch Sonic. We got a much-needed break.

But in all scenarios, the kids had fun. And that's the point of traveling with your kids so that they have fun.

There's a chance you'll have some fun too, but don't hold out for too much hope. Remember, it's about them now and less about you.

With all of the effort, possible pain, and stress of traveling, based on our experiences, I say that it is still worth it. To paraphrase Jessica Biel's character from the classic *Summer Catch*, "If you want big rewards, you gotta take big risks." We have modified it a bit, too; *if you want a bigger life, you have to take on bigger challenges.* Traveling with kids is a challenge. It's easier to stay home. I get that. But go out, make those memories happen, and see that family while you still can. Because you and them will have a story to tell for years to come.

Now, I know I said a few pages ago that family should come to you since traveling with kids is more challenging than adults traveling by themselves. Of course, sometimes it just isn't possible for your family, like when my grandparents were in their late 80s/early 90s, and we took Jake in 2019. Grandma and Grandpa should not have come anywhere near a plane, so we sucked it up and made the trip. And who knows, odds are you will make memories that will last a lifetime.

Like when we were on our Yellowstone trip, having just gotten through airport security with our two toddlers and two grandparents, and found ourselves at the gate where Jake suddenly pulled down his pants. "Put your penis away!" I told him.

"I was just checking to see how big it is," he replied.

See? Those kinds of stories!

Chapter 12

Your Little Petri Dishes

I deas for writing strike me in different ways. At the park with the kids. While eating dinner with the family. Visiting my in-laws.

And like this one, curled up in a fetal position on our bed, trying to get warm and fight off the unrelenting nausea as I shiver with whatever stomach bug my kids brought home from school.

Ah, yes, our little sickness vectors.

Now, I am not an infectious disease expert. I am not a microbiologist. But I am a pharmacist trained to study scientific literature.

I am also an observer of patterns. And based on my observations, your kids will get sick despite your best efforts to avoid risks as in big gatherings. Despite the gallons of hand sanitizer you will wash them in. And if you have multiple kids, they will get each other sick despite trying to keep them from sharing germs.

What are you to do with such a reality? Accept learned helplessness.

I was having a conversation with a neighbor who has two young kids. We were discussing how our respective plans over the past month had been thwarted by a rash of colds, fevers, and various ailments our kids had. And had spread to the rest of the family.

"It's that learned helplessness, I guess," he lamented.

Indeed. Or as Bart Simpson so accurately said once while paraphrasing Homer's life lessons: "Can't win, don't try."

Now, you shouldn't totally give up, and you should try to live a full, fun life with your kids. But you are going to have to start accepting some realities that are well beyond your control. And that is your kids are gonna be sick. My wife likes to quote a statistic I can't back up with evidence that kids get 9-12 colds per year. Seems low.

What the study didn't show was that they always occur when you have big plans, want to travel, and especially if you have booked something that is nonrefundable. I think you should still make plans and still travel. Hell, I wrote an entire chapter on it. But mathematically, you now have one (or more) members of your family you statistically count on to ruin your plans with their illnesses (because you are lovingly taking care of them. Don't forget that part as you weep at the non-refundable airline ticket). It's just more likely to happen.

Like the rest of my excellent dadding advice, you may be waiting for some tips or nuggets of knowledge that will make the reality of when your kid is sick better. There is really nothing as a parent that sucks more than seeing your kid sick (even losing airline tickets, see, I am not that heartless). Here are a few quick hits to prepare you for the inevitable and help you navigate when your kiddo is feeling under the weather:

- Keep them hydrated. You don't need to add electrolyte and fluid complications on top of their already sick state.
- Keep a steady supply of children's Tylenol or Motrin (we use the generic) on hand. We use the dye-free version, but it's your choice if you want to roll the dice with Red Dye #3.
- Now is a great chance for you to use that limited screen time/tablet time with them. My youngest wanted to only watch baseball highlights on his first major illness as a sentient being. On the one hand, I was really bummed he wasn't feeling good. But on the other hand, I couldn't have been prouder.
- The germs shall spread throughout the house. I am not saying lick the doorknobs and share drinks, but I have heard of parents feverishly trying to keep everyone separated, creating a big ball of anxiety on top of the problem of sick kids. Do your best, but there is nothing more disheartening than "doing everything" and still getting sick. Do a reasonable amount and hope for the best.
- If you have multiple kids, odds are they won't be

kind and get sick at the same time. When one goes down, just assume the next two week's plans are off the board. It's better to not hold out hope.

- Now may not be the best time for big, expensive trips overseas. Unless you have money to burn and a good nanny/support system at home that will watch them while they are sick.
- Get a network of people that are willing to watch your kids if they are sick and you need to work.
- Buy travel insurance. As much as it pains me, and I hate wasting money on insurance you typically don't need, stuff will come up. At worst, see if your credit card company offers some travel insurance or trip protection.
- Enjoy the snuggles. Soon enough, they will be brooding, angry, sick teenagers.

In short, the kids will get sick, infect everyone else, and you will have to change your plans, often for weeks at a time. On our first overnight away from Jacob in 2019, he ended up having a stomach bug we were unaware of until my wife spent that first night in our hotel in a shivering, fetal and vomiting position, I spent the next night in such a position, and my parents ended up down for the count for a couple of days (thanks for taking him!). So, even if you escape from your sick kids, they will find a way to get you from afar.

Just remember:

Can't win. Don't try.

Chapter 13

The Kid Looks Like a Ballplayer

s I write this, T-Ball has fired up for our second season. Maybe you are reading this in the dead of winter or perhaps during a sweltering July. Maybe even during the magic of Fall, when everything gets flavored like pumpkin spice, and every Saturday, Sunday, Monday, and Thursday are taken up with the sweet sounds of chronic brain injuries; I mean football. So, while it may not be baseball season right now for you, it certainly is in our house.

Having my kid(s) in T-Ball suits me just fine, as I am a big baseball fan. I played. I enjoy watching it. And based on the commentary I hear at most games I go to ("Just HIT the ball, c'mon!"), I understand the game pretty well relative to the layperson. So, when Cassie was pregnant, and we knew the gender of our baby, I got a lot of comments from people that went something like this:

"What if he doesn't like baseball?"

"I'll bet you hope he likes baseball."

"If he doesn't like baseball, are you going to give him up for adoption?"

The questions were puzzling for me. If he didn't like baseball, of course, Jacob was going to have to find another home. But to really drive home my disappointment in his love for America's Pastime, I would trade him, along with cash considerations, to another family with a kid who did like baseball and a baby to be named later.

Hypothetical kid trade scenarios aside, I understand why people would ask this question. I have seen many a dad live vicariously through their kid to overcome their own athletic failures and shortcomings, regardless of whether or not that kid enjoyed the sport. It made me sad for the kid, the parent, and the coach who had to try to motivate a kid who didn't want to be there in the first place. All the while calming down the overzealous parent who didn't understand why their mopey, apathetic kid wasn't starting at shortstop every game.

It might be because their kid wasn't good enough, but it could also be because their kid didn't try or practice because their kid didn't want to be there.

As a result, I made sure when faced with the above questions to answer them in a way I hope you answer those same questions:

"Whatever they are into, I just want them to work hard to be the best at it that they can."

I mean this with all sincerity. It's easy to say for me, I

guess, 'cuz my kid woke up yesterday for the first T-Ball practice and even put his uniform on to wear to school. I'll get to some tricks to try to help your kid lean toward what you are interested in, in a bit. But you know what? Kids are wired how they are wired. And they kind of like what they like. While Jake loves T-Ball (hitting and the after-game snack, specifically) he also loves drawing, painting, and strumming the guitar, and wants to be an actor instead of going to kindergarten. And my wife and I totally support all of those interests as long as it leads him down a path of mastery of a craft to its fulfillment for optimal enjoyment.

But the kid does look like a ballplayer, right?

Taken March 2022 before Jake's 1ˢᵗ T-ball game.

This is a snapshot of what he is into right now, and as I discussed about toys, preferences can change. Fast. In the wide world of sports, he also likes golf, basketball, football, and, as much as it makes my All-American heart cringe, soccer. Sorry to the rest of the world, but soccer is boring to me. Not even *Ted Lasso* can make me enjoy the sport. And if not for top-notch writing, out-of-this-world acting, and a deep need for something to laugh at after watching, I would have ditched that soccer propaganda long ago.

So, what if my kids want to play soccer?

Let them play soccer. Go watch. Support them. And make sure to bring a good book because if you think soccer is, at its best, impossible to watch, then you have never seen youth soccer before. Yikes.

As I said, I suggest you support your kids in any pursuit they enjoy that teaches them discipline, teamwork, and physical skill. This isn't your life; it's theirs. That is until they grow old enough to be part of club sports. Then their life *is* your life. And your life is going to be nothing but an endless stream of expensive travel to tournaments, paying for hotels, all in the name of the chance for your kids to chase some elusive scholarship when in reality, it is meant to line the pockets of the insidious "club team" organizers.

Play ball?!

Set the Example

I remember as a kid growing up, seeing my dad play racquetball with his friends, golf with his buddies, and an occasional scratcher ticket (which, in all fairness, he picked up from *his* dad). Maybe it was a coincidence that I also ended up playing racquetball, golf, and an occasional scratcher. Feel free to judge, but nothing sets off a road trip like a stop-in for a tank of gas and a two-dollar scratcher that is bound to cover the car floor in "loser dust" after it's scratched.

I also remember, as a kid, the other poor kids being forced to play sports by parents who did not seem interested in any sort of athletic pursuits. That is not to judge the less than athletic, but to highlight that the kids seemed as uninterested in playing sports as their parents were. It was a big bowl of apathy all around. The parents were not engaged, did not seem to care what had happened to them, and did not invest any sort of time or effort into their kids' enjoyment and success.

There are a few of you out there getting frustrated, and I can hear you thinking, "Okay, Mr. Sports-guy, life is not all about sports. What if I want my kid to do something other than sports, you big dumb jock?!"

Point well taken. Nerd.

I kid; I am a nerd, too! I was never great at sports! My dad's athleticism skipped me, and based on my sons' hand-eye coordination and speed, thankfully, at least skipped a single generation. I'll get back to athletic pursuits in a moment, but let's go down the non-sports road for a moment. In 2015, I finally got a guitar, took a few lessons, and began to fill the musical void left in me after I quit piano lessons at six years old because my teacher's house smelled like moth balls. Oh, and I never saw my parents play it or any other musical instrument. My motives for picking up the guitar later in life were multifold. First of all, I just wanted to rock! Secondly, I had dreamed of someday sitting around the campfire and being the person who busted out the songs. Finally, I knew one day I may have kids, and I would want them to play an instrument. I also didn't want to be a hypocrite and say they needed to play one when the best daddy could do was tap his wedding ring on the side of the car with the windows down.

As of now, I am still not great, but I am passable. And to my boys, I am Eric *Friggin'* Clapton. More importantly, when we got our kids guitars, and they saw Daddy playing his, guess what they did? Picked up theirs.

We have had many family jam sessions not because I said my son needed to play guitar, but because he saw me playing, and his mirror neurons kicked in, and he didn't want to miss out.

Now, back to sports.

As I was saying, you want your kid to do something? Then you better give it a shot yourself. I remember it was a spring day in 2021, and I had that baseball itch. No, not the kind where you haven't cleaned your jock strap for a several-game stretch because you are on a winning streak, but one of those "I just need to feel the ball hit my glove" kind of itches. My wife was busy. My dad was not at the house. And the neighbor kids couldn't handle my heat.[26]

So, as sad as this sounds, I just picked up a ball and threw it about 20 feet in the air and caught it. Over. And over. And over again. It filled up something in my soul. But it also sparked something in my oldest son, who saw his

---

[26]   *Okay, it's more like they thought it was weird a grown man was desperately wanting to play catch. They very much could handle my "heat." I never, and currently don't, throw particularly hard.*

dad participating in this strange ritual.

"Can I play some catch with you?"

It may have been the greatest moment of my parenting life up to that point. It was like the ending of *Field of Dreams,* only with more tears of joy and substantially less corn.

The lesson, though, is that I had been asking Jake to play baseball for a long time, and he just hadn't been into it. But, once he saw his old man looking silly tossing that ball in the backyard, he wanted in. And now? Now he wakes up on the first day of T-Ball season, puts on his baseball clothes, and wears them to school. I can't guarantee these kinds of results, but it certainly can't hurt. I will touch on the "careful they're watching" approach a little later in the book, but this copying of your behavior can go both ways. So, make sure they catch you tossing a ball and not tossing all of your life away on your phone.

Make It Fun!

If you are tired of me using the T-Ball example, you may want to skip to the next chapter. On second thought, you know what? I'll use my guitar example too. Oh, ya know what? I can use an example from my comedy career too. Oh, you know what?

Chicken Butt. Made you say it.

Firstly, back to T-Ball. We didn't plan on starting organized sports with our oldest at age three going on four. But our friend was coaching. And our friend is very fun. And from my memories of playing sports at a young age (and all ages, for that matter), baseball can be especially prone to kids abandoning it because it is too boring and hard. While we had a plan to wait, we decided to make the leap a couple of years earlier so the experience would be more likely perceived as a fun activity.

Aaaaaand so that my wife and I could hang out with the other parents we were already friends with. It can't *all* be about the kids, right?

I think the mistake a lot of parents make with youth sports is taking it way, *way* too seriously. And at the age demographic that this book is targeting, expecting way too much. What I loved about the coach of our T-Ball team, and what I tried to convey as an official assistant coach (for tax purposes, those drives to and from practice were a write-off), was to just have fun. Because four to five-year-olds on a T-ball field, or any field or court for that matter, really don't have much context for what is going on. It's why they pick grass, pick their nose, and pick the worst times to have their toddler meltdowns.

Therefore, we ran practices with fun stations that lasted a few minutes at a time, which was just slightly longer than most of the kids' attention spans. Each practice ended with a snack that a parent was responsible for (I could have done without the sugar bombs and the verbal gymnastics required to keep our kid from eating too much garbage), and that's what the kids looked forward to. As a result, there was a lot of enthusiasm.

For Jake, I emphasized the most important parts of baseball to keep it interesting and fun. Getting a bat the same colors as Spiderman, for one. Wearing his pants pulled up to show lots of sock was another. And the thing that kept Jake coming back, game after game: eye black.

There was no real reason he needed to wear it because it wasn't like he was battling mile-high fly balls or staring into the sun while trying to field a bunt with the game on the line. But you know what? It looks friggin' cool, and he was all into it. You know what? He kept coming back. Along the way, he realized hitting was really fun (duh), and so when it came time to see if he wanted to go another year in T-Ball, he couldn't wait to swing his new orange bat (the Spiderman phase had ended, mercifully), and he was devastated when there was no eye black in our bag for the first practice.

For the other kids, I would come up with silly games and interactions to take their minds off the fact that they were actually playing T-Ball, which can be boring for a four-year-old. I tapped one kid's helmet every time they got on base when I was a base coach. When I was the coach putting the ball on the tee, I would move the ball around in my hand and make silly noises, which was fun for the kids, but for me, it meant they were learning to actually look at the ball. They relaxed, laughed, and actually were having fun. Then I hit em' with the very technical hitting advice:

"Watch the ball and swing as hard as you can!"

We didn't keep statistics, but when I was at the hitting station, our team had the fewest swings and misses of any coach. Probably.

On the other hand, sports isn't the only place where making things fun keeps bringing kids back. Remember those guitar jam sessions I mentioned? Well, with any fun activity, there is a way to screw it up. Kind of like youth sports, overcoaching and over-teaching can ruin a kid's interest in something they are enjoying. With Jake playing the guitar, I had to fight my urge to teach him the "right" way to play with chords, strumming, and trying to put it together into a song. But with such a young kid, I realized that if I wanted him to keep playing, we had to keep it fun. Much like my simple T-Ball hitting advice, the guitar advice was similarly simple:

1) Don't slam it down.
2) Try to hold it in your lap.
3) Rock out!

Initially, it was a lot of hard strumming and near slamming down of the guitar. In fairness, based on his expressions, he was following Rule #3. But if his rough treatment of the guitar was to continue, we were soon to not have a guitar for him to Rule #3 all night and party every day. He got past his rough treatment of the instrument. Which was good. He then played guitar like a four-year-old who had never played before. Which was about what you imagine it was. There wasn't much rhythm, rhyme, or reason for what he was playing. But damn, if he wasn't following Rule #3 to the letter!

After he strummed and hummed for a bit, he would ask with a big smile, "Was that a real song?!" Fortunately, my brain is full of '90s Alternative and Country jams, with a healthy smattering of Classic Rock mixed in too. Therefore, whenever he managed to strike a sound that was similar to anything my ears had heard, I quickly shot back with a:

"Closing Time."

"Semi-Charmed Kind of Life."

"Free Fallin.'"

"Gone Country."

This was often met with a beaming smile and an immediate call to my wife of "Mama, I just played a *real* song!"

Hey, it was real to him.

A few days down the line, after his discovery of music, a family member was over. I will protect their anonymity, but Jake was understandably excited to show off his new musical prowess. He got his Jake-sized guitar out, urged the family to gather 'round, and started on his "songs." The response to which was:

"Wow! Let's get you some lessons so you can learn some songs."

Trying to salvage his love and avoid confusion, I loudly, and with a large amount of annoyance, interjected, "To help you learn *more* songs! Because you already know so many. Right **REDACTED**?!"

We've covered sports and music, but you might have heard I am a comedian. Or possibly figured it out based on how much you have been laughing while reading this book. I typically don't like advertising that I am a comedian because if someone then doesn't subsequently laugh at something I say, I find it to be a huge letdown that crushes my already low self-esteem. Anyways, I try to make people laugh, kind of, for a living and kind of, as a hobby.

Like the "Are you going to make them like baseball?" question, a lot of people have asked if I would try to push my kids into doing improv comedy like their old man.

About that, like my other hobbies, I certainly don't want to push them into it. Because I am so hilarious, it's likely, via osmosis, that my kids have already developed a great sense of humor. For toddlers, at least.

But after a few nights of "Daddy is leaving before bedtime to go to improv," Jake started asking, "What is an improv?" and "Can I go with you?"

I started by playing a simple improv game with him and our family, which is called, "Zip Zap Zop." It's a fun, silly game that helps a group of almost any size pass energy around, give the letter Z some love, and is so easy a three-year-old could play it (which is the age Jake started playing with us). Like what I have been emphasizing, we made it fun and loosely followed the rules.[27] It's very simple: one person starts by pointing at someone and saying, "Zip." That person finds someone else, points at them, and says, "Zap." If you are a pattern person, you can guess that the final person finishes with a "Zop," pointing at another person in the circle. The pattern repeats until the group is sufficiently giggled out. It got him interested enough to want to come see a show.

But I wanted to up the fun factor, so I brought him along one night to an "Improv Jam." It's like an improv show; only the audience gets to come on stage and play along as well. We made it a big event, where I picked Jake up from school, and I brought a special snack treat for him (popcorn), and we braved downtown Tucson on a Friday night. He got on stage, warmed up with the group playing

---

27   Here is a link to a video if you want to learn to play "Zip Zap Zop:" https://youtu.be/AZWq4jXNL2E

"Zip Zap Zop" (better than some of the adults!), and then chose to watch me make the magic on stage.

I know he had fun. You know why? As soon as we got in the car, he asked, "Can we go to that again?!"

Mission accomplished. Along the way, I made a point of not overly worrying about the "how" as long as the "what" was "we're having fun." If my kids want to pursue an athletic, musical, or comedy career, there is time to coach them up. I just try to keep them from developing any bad habits or motions when it comes to sports and *let 'em run!* Because nothing sucks the fun out of something for a kid, like being told they are doing it wrong or need to change if they are enjoying it at that moment. The goal at this age, at least for this author and dad, is to just get his kids *into* stuff. Hopefully, it's stuff that I like and can share with my kids, but if not, as long as it is a skill that is useful and productive (and I put athletics and music in that category) and they are having *fun,* it's cool with me. In that case, they will be more likely to stick with it.

Hence, the reasons why I quit piano and soccer. They weren't fun, plus that piano teacher's house smelled like mothballs. I recommend avoiding any mothball-scented scenarios if at all possible.

Chapter 14

Quick Hits of Help

I hope you are enjoying the book so far. The good news? You are over halfway done! The bad news? This chapter is filled with goodies and nuggets I couldn't find a good fit for in my other chapters. But much like dadding, there comes a point when fatigue sets in. Therefore, I have some quicker, shorter hits for your quicker, shorter attention span to help you with a variety of Dad issues, from cranky kids, to food waste, and the ultimate dad uniform!

The Cranky Kid Checklist

Pop quiz, quick! Your kid is crying. They aren't listening. They are throwing a tantrum. What do you do? What DO YOU DO?! Hurry, time is ticking, and they aren't getting any more consolable. The meltdown is imminent, and it is on your shoulders, Dad!

It is during those moments that mere men are made into *dads*. Trying to think your way out of a tantrum will do no good. When the tears (and possibly other bodily fluids) start flying, you have to fall into a muscle memory pattern that helps you stay calm, objective, and effective. The good news is there is a hierarchy that we follow in your house you may find helpful. It goes a little something like this, once your kid starts to get cranky, be sure to check:

Have they eaten?

Many tantrums can be headed off at the pass with a well-timed snack. This is on a kid-by-kid basis, but we know, at least for Jake, once he starts acting like an exceptionally unreasonable turd, it's time to eat something. The challenge is if he goes too long, he will refuse to eat. Don't let this happen to you. Remember, I have provided plenty of healthy, protein-laden options for your snacking readiness. But know that if a kid storm is a-brewin,' any port will do. We aren't going to try and win any "best-fed kids awards" when it's a banana, blueberries, or even a piece of dark chocolate, or a full-blown tantrum. You need to learn based on your own experiences with your kid(s), for example, what the first sign of crankiness can be....

Are they tired?

I'll talk shortly about ending the fun before it goes too far, but think about how you act when you are tired. I bet you can be a bit of a jerk. Well, toddlers haven't learned the emotional regulation you and I have, and don't understand the concept of "tired." If a snack fails to placate them, perhaps it's time to dim the lights and try for some sleep or at least, a nap. And if that doesn't work, then at least some of what we call in our house, "quiet play time." This can mean a puzzle, reading a book together, or, judge if you would like, throwing a show on the TV. Anything to get their tired bodies stationary. Are you tired right now? If you already have kids, I bet you are. Do you get cranky more easily when they don't, and by proxy, *you* don't get a good night's sleep? I bet you do. Do you appreciate it when you are dragging ass, a little down time? I'm not saying I have a gambling problem, but I'll put down some of my hard-earned book royalties that say you do. Make sure your kids get a chance to rest.

👫 Are they experiencing overstimulation?

As a parent, we can sometimes think more is better. More activities. More toys. More choices for what our kids want. But if you have fed them, tried to rest them, and they are still agitated, they may just be overstimulated. Try to think of what life is like as a toddler: you get fed, bathed, changed, toted around. Okay, those all sound pretty sweet. But how about the parts where everything is so new, big, and possibly scary. What, to us, seems like a fun trip to see a Major League Baseball game can actually turn into a sensory overload situation for your kid(s).

At this point, a little dose of empathy, putting yourself in your kid's/kids' shoes, helps. What is the solution after this realization? Unfortunately, if you are having a good time, this means removing them from whatever overstimulation situation that may be. This is not a sexy solution, but an honest one.

👟 Do your kids take their shoes off outside?

I don't care if you live in the desert like me, somewhere

157

in the Midwest, or on the surface of the ocean; if you don't do this, then dust, mud, or coral dust will find its way into them and all over your house. If you want to save money on a vacuum cleaner replacement, I highly recommend making it a practice to remove footwear outside, or at the very least, if your house is fortunate enough, to have a mud room or similarly designated space.

⏰ **Remember when you couldn't just wait until the last minute to grab your things and get out the door?**

Me neither. Kids are not privy to what my wife and I refer to as "clock time." As in, you can say, "We need to leave by 8:00," and as far as your kid(s) go, that means it's time to look for the lost Lego piece to fix their car (hint: it's under the couch). What I will remind you, and what my wife reminds me of, is that with kids, it just takes longer to get ready than you think. This part is easy to understand. The more challenging part is keeping your cool and not getting frustrated or angry, especially at the kids. Remember, it's not their fault *you* didn't pull out. So don't take your frustration out on them. Instead, build more time into your routine, pack up things the night before you go somewhere, and let go of the need to be on time everywhere. Hell, part of the reason I had kids was so that I could make excuses for either being late or not showing up to places I didn't really want to go to anyways.

🛒 **Do you own a wagon?**

I am not talking about a little red wagon. Wagons these days are like automobiles: they have more technology in them than we could ever believe. We first got privy to the idea when our neighbor brought her daughter, a cooler, and a tray of food over in one for a party we had. My wife and I were intrigued but overwhelmed at the options staring us down on Amazon. Single vs double-decker? Do we get a shade? An extra handle/storage area for pushing. It was true *paralysis by analysis*. When T-Ball season and we were the only suckers lugging food, gear, and a toddler in our arms, we knew it was time to hop into action. It has been one of our best parenting investments and may have more miles on it than our 2004 GMC Yukon XL.

What's your "dad uniform"?

I spent the first 25 years of my life trying to dress cool. Then I met my wife, she loved me for me, and the effort abruptly stopped. Now, being a dad isn't a license to look like a slob. I still keep my stained sweatpants/shirt at home when it's daycare pickup time. But there is a level of practicality you should exercise with having kids: They need to be able to see you. What does that look like? We're bringing the '90s back!

We're talkin' neon, baby.

Going on a walk or a bike ride and want to make sure cars can see you and your kids?

Neon.

Heading to the park and want to give your kids the freedom to roam but still find you?

Neon.

Taking a family trip through the airport and worried the airline will be desperate for someone to help load bags onto the plane?

Neon.

While you don't have to get all neon'd out, I have found that I enjoy the different shades, it brings back fond memories of my childhood, and my kids can see me easier. I wear a bright shirt and, when traveling, bright calf-high socks since my kids can't exactly see that high in a sea of adults. Will you look a little ridiculous? Yes. But this will come in handy when your kids are teenagers and you really want to embarrass them. "You look stupid, Dad!" They'll complain.

But you can just fire back with, "I have been dressing this way since you were a kid, and you used to appreciate how visible I was. I am just trying to hold onto a little piece of your sweet innocent youth. Do you really want to take that away from me?"

At which point, they will say yes, and ask you to drop them off a block before you get to school. Just think of all the gas money you'll save over the lifetime of middle and high school!

Those neon socks are going to pay for themselves in no time.

Along those lines, dress your kid in neon too. When we are out for a hike, Jake likes to push the boundaries of independence and run far ahead of us. No problem, because in his bright neon orange shirt, we could see him far up the trail. Putting your kids in bright colors becomes a sort of reverse *Where's Waldo* situation where spotting your kid in the crowd is actually easier. This logic also works out well when they start riding their bikes and generally venturing near roads and parking lots. Just assume that most people driving their cars are checking their phones while hopped up on some sort of pharmaceutical and will need every advantage to brake safely and quickly enough. Parenting is all about stacking the deck in your favor, so find some of the loudest clothes that 1992 would be proud of and cover your kid in them.

✋ When should you end the fun?

Have you ever heard of the Great Wolf Lodge? It is an indoor waterpark that is franchised around the country. Our family took a trip there with our two and four-year-olds. It was awesome. The kids loved every part of the experience, but not surprisingly, the water park itself was their favorite. They showed no fear in going down slides, playing in the wave pool, and shootin' some pool hoops.

Which is exactly why we ended our days there early.

"How could you be so cruel as to take away the joy of kids so soon?" Some of you overly sensitive and kid-centric dads may be asking. "They were having fun, and you RUINED it for them!" You might be complaining.

Wow, an exclamation point? Now, you are getting needlessly aggressive.

I'll refer you back to the bullet point about the steps of dealing with a misbehaving kid. Two of those involved kids being either too tired or too overstimulated, both of which can easily happen in a water park scenario. In our experience, even if your kids are having an amazing time doing something, it is better to pack it up too early rather than let them get overtired or overstimulated.

The key is leaving on a happy note before they become

unruly and undo all of the good and fun that was had. We exhibited the same tactic at the kids' first Major League game we took them to. We spent most of the time at the Diamondbacks' kids' area, letting them hit wiffle balls and climb over the playground, watched about 1.5 innings of actual baseball from our seats, and when that game became official at five innings, we hit the road. Beyond big events like baseball games and water parks, we have used this tactic for birthday parties, family events, or any activity where going too long was likely going to end in a meltdown.

While you may say this is mean, let me ask you, "When do you recall something fun you were doing at four years old that ended too early, and it scarred you for life? For that matter, when do you recall doing *anything* at four years old?"

My point exactly. Cut off the fun before the meltdown and save your sanity. In other words, end the fun too early rather than too late.

⟳ Can you pivot?

As a dad, your goal is to instill good habits in your kids so that when they turn 18, they can get their asses out of your house, and you can finally live in peace. Oh, and to create good, productive, tax-paying citizens. As such, the habit-building begins as their sentience grows in toddlerhood. The good news is with a lot of hard work and diligence, you will be able to help mold their behaviors. For example, we actually turned Jake into a productive member of the household and had him do some basic chores like putting his laundry away and helping put the silverware away in the dishwasher. But as soon as that milestone was reached, he regressed on the bad habit of wanting a snack after we had done our bedtime routine of snacks, stories, and brushing our teeth. Beyond it being a path to an adulthood of obesity, it was significantly cutting into Cassie's and my sleep time when each night, he slowly munched on something the way a cow chews on cud.

When coming back out of bed, claiming how hungry he was, it meant a new snack and resetting the time it took to get him to sleep. So while we had a helper with the laundry and dishes, we were looking at one to two hours less sleep each night. We worked on fixing his snacking habits, and it rolled into a problem of him wanting to bring his toys to show off at school. So it went, and so it shall go for you as well. Just accept that your life will be a never-ending game of habit fixing. Much like a leaky roof, the process won't end, you will lose sleep, and your patience will become non-existent.

👫 How do you and your kids make new friends?

Meet on Neutral Ground. Maybe your kid will make friends at school or daycare or wherever you house them while you attempt to be a productive member of society and earn a living. Get used to new friends, playdates, and the weird parents that created the little monsters your kids want to share their time with. Cassie and I have been unusually fortunate to have an incredible network of friends that we knew before we all reproduced at approximately the same time. So there have been minimal "new friend" experiences. Again, count us in the fortunate category that all of the new friends we have made share similar values, approaches to raising kids, and have a decent sense of humor about the parenting approach. I am sure they will totally love this book. In fact, if you want to avoid the "neutral ground" strategy, just give the dad a copy of this book and see what he thinks. If he likes it, he is cool to hang out wherever. If that's not possible, then I recommend...

Making the first meeting on a neutral site. Like the Superbowl, if one team's fans are unruly, weird, or downright rude (looking at you, Eagles fans), there is not the added irritation of them wrecking your sacred home field. With a new family, you never know what they could be into food-wise, habit-wise, toy-wise, or space-wise. What if you bring your famous jerky, and they are vegan? What if they overly utilize plug-in scents in their house, and the smell gives you a headache? What if their kids have super cool expensive toys that make your kid jealous and hate you?

You can't risk that for a new friend. So, meet at a neutral site. Parks are great. It gives the kids a chance to play; if something gets broken, the only ones paying for it are the taxpayers. And there is something that you may need to utilize if you realize this will not be a lasting friendship-space.

If you are in your house, you can't just tell these weirdos to go without just cause. And if you are at someone else's house and things are going bad, you better be quick to come up with an excuse to leave or at least have one chambered and agreed upon by the spouse. Of course, this will only teach your kids that lying is okay. And we just talked about good habits. Plus, you want to save the "white lie" card for something more important, like getting out of a traffic ticket or explaining to another parent why their kid isn't getting enough playing time when you are the coach. But at a nice big park, if your kids and you organically just drift to the other side and out of sight, it's just the nature of free play. Also, you want to foster independence and creativity, right?

So if things go bad, you have some room to roam and hide. If they go well, you establish rapport and some basic principles of kid rearing you agree on (what to feed them, what they can watch, who you vote for), then feel free to take that playdate relationship to the next level and have them over to your house. Otherwise, you can just chalk this up to another day at the park and never speak of those weirdos who met you there again.

🎵 Remember when your dad would aggressively reside over the thermostat?

Do you remember how odd and unreasonable it seemed? Well, you were wrong to think that way. Whatever it is about having half of your DNA staring at you in life form, maybe it's a financial thing, maybe it's a control thing, but you too will be changing the temperature in your house. The moment that umbilical cord is cut, you will have the urge to remind the new child that until they start paying the electric bills, they can just leave the temperature alone.

Same goes for leaving lights on in rooms people aren't in. To make this transition to fatherhood easier, I suggest indoctrinating your kid(s). My oldest now will turn off lights that have been left on while yelling, "We're wasting juice!" Does my wife get upset that sometimes she is in the room with the light that is turned off? Sure. And I just ask her if she hates the planet, wasting resources, and wants an apocalyptic resource-poor future for our kids. Or if her comfort or "ability to see while using the bathroom" are more important than a bright future for our potential grandkids. The answer, based on her angry screams, is "Yes."

What about food waste?

On the subject of waste, there will likely also be an obsessive need to not waste food/finish whatever is left over from your kid's/kids' meals. Adjust your portions down or your pant sizes up accordingly.

What's my last "Dad Hack?"

It consists of a broad recommendation for approaches to all things with kids. Don't put too much energy into everything. Rather, let things unfold as they do and let the kids react as they do. Pardon the many T-Ball examples, but I am writing this during the spring. It's on my mind. But so many parents build up playing. Going to practices. Getting the team's jerseys and shirts (put that money in a 529!), saying how much fun it will be, living and dying with each play. Meanwhile, the kid pretty much cares about three things: the post-game snack, the grass, and various ways to throw dirt in the air. Basically, anything but T-ball. I can't blame them for it; it's a terrible brand of baseball. Fortunately, as a Cubs fan, I am used to such subpar play.

However, psychologically speaking, the return never meets the buildup. Whether we are five-year-olds going to T-Ball, or 35-year-olds looking forward to our Maui vacation, some of the greatest moments in life are the ones that take us by surprise without much buildup. That's what I recommend with kids. I can't tell you how disappointed adults get when they talk up some experience for their kid(s) (sports, Santa, a show), and the response, at best, is, "Meh." I have had much better success with keeping the plans vague, downplaying what is to come, or straight-up surprising them. The variable reward model that keeps adults glued to Twitter and casinos doesn't just start when you hit puberty. Use it to your advantage with kids.

Plus, all the energy you adults put out gives me anxiety. Imagine what it does to your kids' unformed prefrontal cortexes.

Chapter 15

Money, Money, Money

s subjective and ever-changing as raising kids can be, there are a few objective things you really should have in place, like "getting your ducks in a row," as the kids say or is it as the old people say? In any case, here are a few things you really need to have lined up if you are planning to have kids or already have kids.

You're gonna die. So am I. So are we all. I hope not for a long time, for your sake and your kids' sake. But nothing is promised.

An acquaintance's spouse passed away a few years ago, leaving behind two kids, a mortgage, and an unfilled application for life insurance. As hard as it was for that spouse to lose their partner and for their kids to lose their parent, it made matters more complex having to figure out their financial footing without one of their providers.

Death is not pleasant to think about, especially for a toddler who realizes their mortality. If you think I have a great tip for handling that discussion, I am sorry to say I will stick to the jokes and leave the heavy talk for you to figure out. But should it come to you early, with a wife and kid(s) to take care of, having a life insurance policy in place will not take away their emotional pain but will help alleviate a big slice of stress at the very least. How much should you get? What kind of policy is best? Oh boy, that is a question for a financial expert and/or professional. Plus, if I gave specific financial advice out, I am pretty sure I would have to have some sort of disclaimer to keep lawyers away.

As a result, I won't give specific advice on specific life insurance policies and how much money to have on your policy. But there are two basic kinds: whole life insurance and term life insurance. One is expensive, often gives a large commission to the person who sells it to you, and was what my wife and I had before we had a "financial awakening" in 2017. The other is term life which is generally much more affordable and freed up enough money in our budget to save for a down payment on the house I am typing this from. The choice is yours, but I'll say one of the few things that gets my nearly unflappable wife frothy and angry is reminding her of the money we threw away on whole life insurance.

If you are planning on getting your wife knocked up, it's probably a good idea to have a policy on her, too. My wife has one, which is good because she's the one who brings home the bacon in our house. That is unless this book goes gangbusters. Either way, we both sleep better at night, knowing we are covered should one of us meet our early demise. And just so Cassie doesn't get any wild ideas, I periodically (randomly) have one of those true crime shows on, and always emphasize how "I didn't think she'd get away with it!" That's what is called insurance for your insurance.

On the topic of meeting your demise, another order of business with having kids is having someone in place to step in, in case both you and your partner, for lack of a better word, die. Again, we don't plan on this, and it's not fun to think about, but you know what's less fun to think about? You dying and your kids getting raised by The State. That's adding injury to injury.

Perhaps you have a sibling you know would be a kickass (or is currently a kickass) parent, and they are willing to take on the burden of raising your kid(s). Or maybe you don't, but you have some awesome friends that you trust with your kid(s). In our case, if Cassie and I go down, our kids will be going to friends of ours, the guy whom I've known since I was ten. They are a regular part of ours, and our kids' lives, and should something happen to us, we'd sleep well for eternity knowing those two would instill similar values, have the fortitude to handle parenting, and are also well-embedded and connected with our families so they'd keep our kids connected to their biological family.

Now is where you may be hoping for a checklist of how to choose the best "Just in Case" parents. I think this is a conversation you need to have with your spouse. Then, upon agreement, with the possible parents-to-be. And don't be pissed if they say, "No." It's possibly a big burden to take on. For us, with each kid we added to the mix, we worried they'd finally come to their senses and decline as the potential burden grew. Thankfully, we chose people with high character to care for our kids in the event we are not around. A little tip, we made the possible hurt less by highlighting both our respective life insurance policies, and that they'd be named beneficiaries if we both were gone. If you are going to ask someone to care for your kid(s), the least you can do is set them up as financially well as possible.

Speaking of "financially," it is a good idea to be as solid money-wise as possible. That being said, if everyone waited until they were totally "ready" financially, the world would have no kids. There is a balance between having your first kid at the age of 17 with no money or money-making skills and waiting until you are 47 and have an eight-figure net worth. However, once you decide to have kids, and especially once that pregnancy test has two lines/shows positive/has a baby puppet pop out of it, it is a wise choice to save up some cash.

There will be expenses like the actual hospital bill, diapers, wipes, and countless other baby crap you think you need, won't need, but will buy anyways, and the possible loss of income while one or both of you stay home with your new baby. I can't really offer much more specific advice than that, but in the appendix of the book, I'll provide some of my favorite financial resources to help build your money foundation. I can tell you having kids really kick-started my self-education on personal finance, and because of it, I have been able to work part-time, spend more time with my kids, and have enough mental bandwidth left over to write this book. Lucky you.

Chapter 16

Dude "Self-Care"

At first, this chapter was going to be all about the importance of you and the momma of the baby, maintaining a solid relationship, a "foundation" if you will, from which your ability to be a solid dad can stem from and stand on. Then I thought about the single dads out there kickin' ass, and how I didn't want to insult them. Then I thought about the married/relationship'd dads that hold it down while their other half is gone a lot of the time, presumably for work but possibly maintaining a nearly impossible cover for an affair. But it's probably the first one, guys. Then I thought about how we dudes don't really take care of ourselves much. Then I realized this chapter could be a combination of self *and* relationship care, and since I am the author, I get to choose.

What can I say? I aim to please.

As they often (okay, always, legally) announce on flights, if the cabin loses pressure and you are traveling with young kids, you put your own mask on first so that you are conscious and capable of helping the younger person. I think this is good advice and a nice metaphor for how we should take care of ourselves. Also, if you have been flying with or around little kids that are being little shits and wondered if the cabin lost pressure if you would just put that mask on yourself and not the kids just to get them to be quiet, you are not alone, and you are not a monster. It's just a thought. Right? RIGHT?!

Becoming a parent means being selfless and sacrificing for your kids. It can leave you with a pretty empty tank at the end of the day. And for the most part, I think this is good. Parents have become pretty narcissistic and selfish, in my observation, and forgotten that becoming a parent means making sacrifices. Giving up some of this selfishness is a good thing, but like any good thing, it can be taken too far. So far that your own health and well-being can suffer.

It's 2023 as I write this, and the term "Self-Care" is pretty buzzy. I don't know about you, but when I hear self-care, I think of cucumbers over the eyes, days at the spa, and massages. It's not that men can't put vegetables over their eyes. I am personally for anything that will help slow down these Crow's Feet of mine. But the term is not exactly appealing to dudes. On the other hand, taking care of yourself is important. Because if you break down physically or mentally, you aren't going to be able to take care of your kids as well. Then, in 25 years, they will resent you for it. Oh, hell, in 25 years, they will resent you for something anyways, but you might as well take care of yourself along the way.

What does "Dude Self-Care" look like? I think it depends on you and what you like. For many guys, Saturdays and Sundays during football season, hanging out with some bros, and watching other dudes give each other CTE is "self-care." For others, it's wrenching on a car together. Maybe it's a round of golf or a morning at the gym, a round of video games after the kids are asleep, or dusting off that guitar to learn a new song.

I suppose I could keep listing things, but you get the idea. Some common themes I have seen with dads that keep it together, take care of themselves, and kick ass at raising their kids are:

- **Totally getting away from the wife and kids:** This is not meant to be mean or disparaging to our families. But damn, sometimes you gotta get the hell away and hit a reset button. My dad and his friends have been doing a yearly golf trip for 30 years. I was finally invited as an adult in 2016 and saw how much these old dudes looked forward to seeing each other... and getting away.

- **Male social bonding:** That trip reminded me of another common theme, hanging with other dudes and talking dude stuff. While a golf trip may be beyond your grasp, it could also mean gathering at the guy's house (who has a pool table for a night) or working on a project together. My father-in-law does a hunt (or several) each year with his friends. They don't always kill something I get to eat, but he always enjoys his time away from the family and with his friends.

- **Doing something engaging:** I almost said work can be a self-care activity, and some days with my toddlers, it does feel like an escape, but it's not always super engaging. For me, it can be something like repainting a wall or pulling weeds. I find physical work to be engaging and wildly satisfying, but it could be rocking an instrument or getting lost in the world of video games (just don't make this one too long. I am not personally a fan of video games, but I also know many of you are not *personally* fans of physical activity).

- **Doing a physical activity:** Sorry, couch potatoes, but want to be there for your kids? Want to set a good example? I'll let a few football Sundays slide, but you also need to move your ass. Do what is fun, but do something. I promise, at the end of whatever you are doing, you will feel better and be stronger for your family.

The great thing about taking care of yourself? It does not need to take a long chunk of time, which is good because your kids will not allow for that. Your sense of time will get recalibrated, and what you need to refill your tank with will take less and less as you get more and more worn down by those little turds. Therefore, when I sneak a 20-minute nap in, I feel like a brand-new person. Thirty minutes of exercise has me feeling like Rocky at the end of a long training montage. And when I get to hang out with the guys in my neighborhood for a short walk around the neighborhood or an afternoon project at someone's house, it feels like I got multiple days off.

In short, it doesn't take much to take care of yourself, but you will build the foundation to be better for your kids and spouse. Oh, and make sure that spouse of yours gets their self-care too. Moms (at least the good ones) are the most selfless people on the planet, to their own detriment. Trust me, you'll be happier in the long run giving them an afternoon doing whatever the hell it is that women do to care for themselves. My guess is that it does involve some sort of cucumber eye-coverings.

Speaking of those spouses, part of the foundation of raising kids also comes in keeping your relationship strong. To those single Dads/divorced Dads/Dads for whom this advice is not relevant, feel free to fast forward to the next section. Or stick around. I am not the boss of you. Your kids are!

Having a solid relationship can really help when the nights get long, the sleep gets short, and the tension gets, um, tense. Ideally, you and your partner have had time to grow together, come up with a parenting approach you both agree with, and have your relationship in a good place. Because, as I talked about in "Reasons Not to Have a Kid," bringing a new life into this world is not going to fix whatever may be broken in your relationship. It will only exacerbate it.

If you think you'll have time to make your relationship stronger once you have a baby-turn-toddler, you are only fooling yourself. Forging and maintaining a strong bond with your spouse is one of the hardest challenges my wife and I have faced, especially after having kids. Is it because kids have unearthed some deep rifts between us? Made us realize there are things about each other we wished were different? Opened a space/time portal that has us questioning our choices in life?

Well, that third one is only kind of true sometimes in the middle of the long nights and stretches of sickness.[28]

It's mostly because the time and mental bandwidth we used to have to spend on each other, even just as a couple, has been squeezed out, pulverized, and probably peed on by our two sons and newborn daughter. It has become a running joke in our house for Cassie and I to lie down in bed at night, exhausted from the day of toddler wranglin' and work, and sarcastically say to each other:

"Good morning."

Before we can spend five minutes talking about our day, we are asleep. Forget emotional needs, we are just trying to get by sometimes. I am not saying we are going to get divorced because of these challenges, but we do talk about them (when we get the precious time to do so). However, the high divorce rate in the country does make some sense. People spend so much time rearing their kids that they neglect their relationship with their spouse, wake up one day, and realize that they have drifted apart.

Aside from hiring a good divorce attorney, what are you to do?

Rather than accept a slow, miserable decline in your relationship, I recommend (and by "I," I mean my wife, who has contributed to this chapter with her advice too) scheduling time for you and your significant other. In fact,

---

28   *If my kids are reading this later in life: We love you!*

just the other day, after a bit of a tiff the two of us had after some especially challenging days, we realized that we scheduled everything except time together:

- Work
- Dropping and picking kids up from school
- T-Ball
- Playdates
- Dentist appointments

If something is not scheduled, it probably is not going to get done. Therefore, take the time to *schedule time* with your partner. It could be a walk in the evening, a dinner date, or a weekend trip away from the kids. But it needs to be a priority even if it's a few hours a week. Find a babysitter. Lean on your family. Leave your kids at home with enough food and water for a couple of hours (I am kidding, although it does sound appealing at times), and make sure to connect with the one you love (remember, you DO love them).

These times together will strengthen your relationship, refresh you, and make you a better parent. It's like that self-care we talked about, except for both of you. And if you think that 50 bucks for a babysitter is expensive, I'm going to guess it's much less than the divorce attorney you'll be hiring and the child support you'll be paying if you can't keep your relationship together. That time together and money spent is what we call a high return on investment.

How Can You Do It All?

You don't because you can't!

Career, hobbies, health, friends, family, chores, and

sleep. These are all worthy uses of your time. Worthy uses you will have less time to engage in. Kids will not only suck your time, but also your energy. So if you think that at the end of a long day of working, preparing meals for your kids, cleaning up after your kids, playing with your kids, and putting your kids to bed, that you are going to have the mental fortitude to hop into that side hustle, or learn to play the guitar, you will be sorely disappointed.

While this is not a bad thing... because being a dad is amazing. Right? RIGHT?! There is just not much left in the tank at the end of a long day. The best approach is just to accept it. It took a long time for me to be able to. I sometimes sit around and get frustrated, remembering how back in college or during our pre-kid marital days, I would think of something I wanted to do, and then just like...do it. When my goals weren't being achieved, I kept getting angry with myself and wondering, "What's wrong with me?" That's when my wife reminds me, with the point of a finger directed at our kids, what has changed.

Oh. Right.

I like to think of all the obligations of life as levers. Before kids, there is a lot of room to pull down many of those levers at once and do so much more. Kids put a governor on the number of levers to pull, and you just aren't going to be able to do everything you once did.

So which levers to pull? That's up to you to prioritize. But my observation is that if you can get one task done a day for you on top of all your other parenting and life responsibilities, you are doing well.

My advice is to have some grace with yourself, and

accept you are just not going to be able to do as much as you used to anymore. Or try to do it all and burn yourself out because I'm not the boss of you.

When Do You Get Anything Done?

I could hear some frustration from you as you read that last section. "So you're saying you can only expect to really get one thing done a day, but you have written two books, work at least a part-time job, keep a sleek physique, and all of this while raising three kids. How did you do it, Dr. Hypocrite?"

You are correct. I do manage to pack a lot into a day and externally get a lot done. Internally, I feel I leave an embarrassing amount on the table every day. However, I do think that objectively I am able to get a solid amount done on a daily basis. What is my secret? That thing that sets me apart and can set you apart to get your own shit done?

Early mornings or late nights.

What is so magical about these times of the day? It's that, ideally your kids are asleep and can't interrupt you. You want time to yourself? You better plan to work around their sleep schedules. That means getting up at 4:30 as I did today to write this section and then do a quick 20-minute HIIT spin on the Peloton. Okay, it's actually a $200 spin bike from Amazon. And I actually get the Peloton App free from my health insurance. Okay, it's actually not free, it's subsidized by all of the other health insurance premiums. But my frugalness saved us $1500 that I was able to spend on a batting cage for my kids. See how selfless I am?

On the other hand, if you are a night owl, it means getting after your personal pursuit once your kids are asleep.

Whether you work in the morning or evening depends on a couple of factors:

1. *When* do you perform better? And your particular preferences.
2. *When* do/does your kid(s) sleep? And frankly, for how *long*?

The truth is it really only depends on factor two. You think your kid's/kids' sleep schedule cares if you aren't a "morning person?" I guess you're a dad now. Your personal preferences mean *nothing*. So get used to doing stuff when it's least conducive to your circadian rhythm and comfort. Sorry for the bad news, but parenting is all about adaptation. Adapting to your kids' personalities. Adapting to getting less done than you were used to before your kid(s) came into the picture. Adaptation to when, for instance, you (need to adapt or) give your greedy, poor sleeping kid(s) away so you can finally (adapt and) finish your projects. I mean adaptation to new timelines and setting reasonable expectations for balancing the soul-sucking job of parenting with any possibility of personal pursuits.

Of course, if you have a ton of money, you can just throw it at the problem, hire babysitters and childcare during the day, and stay as productive as ever. Hopefully, this productivity will be lucrative for you to pay for the therapy for both you and your kids later in life as you lament, "Cats in the Cradle" style, the time you missed out when they were young and not bitter about your absenteeism.

Are You Doing It Right?

Being a good dad can be subjective. There is no standardized test to know if you are on the right track. And as a student of the early 2000s, all I know is how to take standardized tests. Therefore, it can be frustrating to be left wondering if you are "leaving it all on the field" as a dad. Fortunately, I got some wisdom from a neighbor of ours. She happens to be a mom, but I'll take parenting advice wherever I can, even if this is a book for dads.

We were over at their house, where they had two boys about the same age as our boys. Fortunately, all four kids were playing happily and contentedly while the parents sat around, getting a mental break from being totally "on." One of the most isolating things as a parent can be wondering alone if you are doing a good job. And my wife brought up that curiosity and the fact that we, two parents, are so damn tired all the time. She was asking if they felt the same way, as if we were doing something wrong by being so tired.

Our friend's response sums up the approach of good parenting in an elegantly simple way:

"If you aren't tired, you are doing it wrong."

There you go, a simple heuristic to know if you are doing the best you can as a dad. If you are tired, worn down, and have nothing left at the end of the day, you are probably doing something right. It means you are giving your kids and spouse all you have, which is the point of having kids. That you are now selfless. That they get priority. That when you go to a waterpark, it is they who are shepherded to the fun while you watch and make sure they are safe in the water and while you handle the snacks and sunscreen, and pay for it all or share the cost with your spouse.

While being tired doesn't guarantee good behavior, habits being fixed, or some elusive future college scholarship, it does help prove to yourself that you are doing all you can to be as good of a dad as you can. And that's all your kids can ask for.

Even though it will never be enough for them, which you should just accept as well.

Chapter 17

I Didn't Want to Write This Chapter

B y now, you are nearing the end of the book. I promise. Of course, you have likely read a book before and could tell by the pages you are more done than not.

The title of the chapter sounds ominous, like I have some earth-shattering awful news for you. Don't worry. Or maybe you should.

But the truth is, it is Friday at 9:30 PM. We had T-Ball practice, and the season starts tomorrow. I have felt run down all week. I tried to write last night, but instead, I went to bed at 8:30 (PM if you needed me to be precise). I haven't had a long conversation with my wife in two weeks.

I am just tired. I am a dad. I work a part-time pharmacist job, share kid-rearing duties with my wife, am building a speaking business, writing three newsletters a week, am trying to write this book, and on top of that, my kids are having trouble sleeping.

My tank is empty, and I don't feel like writing right now. While you may not be a celebrated writer. Or like me, a mostly obscure writer, there will come a point when whatever it is you used to want to do or feel like doing won't be what you want to do. You may not realize how empty your tank is until you sit down, glaze your eyes, and try to be productive but instead, hit the refresh button on your social media channels and wonder where the last 35 minutes had gone (I speak from, um, very recent experience.)

Being a dad is hard and draining, and despite it sometimes being rewarding, you will need a break. It's okay. So I asked my parents to pick our kids up from school once a week and feed them dinner so my wife and I could have some time to be together, make simple logistical plans, and get a moment of peace. Trust me, even a two-hour, kid-free block with a fellow adult can feel like a week's vacation.

While you are a superhero to your kids and wife (hopefully, with the help of this book), you need to fill your tank. Don't be ashamed. I am putting the keyboard down after this and going to bed. And when the chance presents itself after you have worn yourself out, you should too.

No, really. GO TO BED.

This book will be here tomorrow for me to write now and for you to read later.

Chapter 18

Raisin' Em Right

W hat is the ultimate goal of having kids? For some, it's having bragging rights for the coolest ways to show off on social media. For others, it's living vicariously through their kid(s) to have their dreams come true.

For me, and what I will suggest for you: raise these little turds into good citizens and have some fun along the way. "Raising kids right" can come in many flavors, forms, and traditions. I am not here to preach to you about "the right way" to raise kids because there are many ways to mold these human lumps of clay into adults. But you are reading a book on being a better dad, so my guess is you are in the market for at least a little advice. So here are a few practical pieces of advice to help raise them up right.

They Won't Listen to You

How about this piece of truth to set the mood to

"bummer?" While this book is geared towards ages "contemplating" to five, I am pretty sure this will ring true for their whole lives. But the same will be true for you someday when you fall victim to "PBS." I am not talking about an inherent love of public broadcasting, but rather "Powdered Butt Syndrome," wherein as the parent, you will never listen to someone whose butt you have powdered/cleaned. Cassie and I both have parents who we have tried to help change some poor dietary habits. Both ignored the advice of their highly educated children. Both then made changes after they saw an article on MSNBC/Fox News, respectively (our parents come from different political backgrounds and yet get along great) about what we had been trying to talk to them about. There is indeed hope for us all. While we were grateful for their changes, it highlighted the fact that those closest to you won't listen to you.

And so it will go for your kids. You know what they should be eating. You know they need to sleep. You know that getting outside and playing sports and being active is good for you. You know that cultivated interests in cool things instead of video games and *Paw Patrol* will lead to a richer life for them. But they don't care what you know.

Basically, kids will be influenced by other people. That's why you need to cultivate relationships with other cool and interesting people in your life. There are a number of ways to go about it. For example, if your own family falls short in some areas, or you just don't have any/many siblings who will be there to be the "cool" aunt or uncle, just incorporate some of your more interesting friends as "Aunt" or "Uncle."

Our kids have an "uncle" who was a professional baseball player turned firefighter. They think he's the coolest and always try to impress him. No matter what I can't get them to do, Cool Uncle TJ can convince them it's time to read for bed, to swing harder at a baseball, or to play a game of soccer to work on their quickness skills.

In an effort for intergenerational appreciation, I think getting some bonus grandparents whenever you can is great too. We have a few neighbors who, to put it kindly, are pretty old, but who have also lived interesting lives, ranging from flying planes to owning a fishing business in Alaska. So having some cool grandparent-like figures has been awesome for our kids.

Along the lines of growing your "family," to gain help or support when needed, when you can't get your kids excited about something, lean on those outside of the walls of your house. For example, right now, our oldest, Jake, loves T-Ball. He has been pumped for T-ball since last year when we got him started. Was it his old man, the big baseball fan, that got him excited? Sadly, but realistically, no.

We were even going to give it a couple of years before enduring the mishigas of youth sports, but our friend, known in this book as "Coach Mark," because his name is Mark and he is the T-Ball coach, was starting a team for his daughter and said that I would be helping him coach and Jake would be playing. Rather than argue, I gave the league my hard-earned money and the T-Ball Giants three months of my time. I agreed because I knew how much fun Coach Mark was going to make the experience for the kids, including my kid.

Guess what? It worked. Jake had a blast the whole season, not because his dad or mom pushed him into it, but because, organically, Coach Mark made the practices and games fun, light, and an event to look forward to. In fact, T-Ball was so fun Henry started participating in practices and games even though he wasn't even two years old. Such is the beauty of positive peer pressure. Someday, when Jake gets that big first-round draft pick signing bonus, I'll buy Coach Mark a beer. He'll get a shot if Henry makes the show too.

But it doesn't have to be organized sports where outside influence can make a difference. Jake's Uncle TJ, the baseball-playing firefighter, got Jake to do something I had been trying for months: push-ups. All it took was the outside influence to make a game of doing push-ups (while playing a game of soccer), and Jake was all in.

As a dad, you are going to want so much for your kids, and because you are reading this book, you are going to want to try so hard too. That's admirable! But working smarter rather than forcing it, relying on the cool people in your life, and backing off the energy a bit will go a long way into helping shape your kids and their habits.

And if that doesn't work, you can always pay a stranger to come to the park and start playing the sport you want your kid to get interested in. Parents have done less ethical things. Probably.

Raise em' Tough

I realize "tough" can conjure up a lot of images for your

kids and what you think that means for them. Does making them tough mean they'll be a bouncer? A cage fighter? A customer service representative for Southwest Airlines?[29]

Perhaps some of those fates are in the cards for your kids. But what I am talking about is not going through life afraid of everything. It's important to be willing to take some risks and fail, to understand that bumps and bruises are just the tax we pay for some of life's most rewarding experiences. I think one of the worst fates you can seal for your kids is to make them scared of anything and everything in the world.

Fortunately for you, Dad, there are some simple things you can do to help *up* your kid's toughness-game, or at least, avoid being afraid of their shadow.

Therefore, watch out when saying the word "careful."

Before I go deeper into the perils of the word "careful," I thought I was super clever and had come up with the concept of being "careful with using the word, 'careful.'" While I contend that I was saying it before the wise Ryan Holliday blogged about it, I must give him credit for an excellent post he wrote for *The Daily Dad,* where he extols the perils of overusing "careful."[30]

Great. Now that you have read a writer with millions more readers than me explaining the concept, let me give it my own spin.

There are a few things wrong with saying "careful" over

---

29   *Don't let the loose dress code and lighthearted image fool you. When passengers get their flights canceled, you gotta be tough on the inside.*
30   https://dailydad.com/be-careful-of-telling-them-to-be-careful/   *As an aside,* The Daily Dad *is an excellent follow for any dad or mom really. It's listed in my recommended resources at the end of the book.*

and over again. In Ryan's post, he says how saying it will put "A voice of nervousness and worry and anxiety. A voice that prevents them from trying and risking. A voice that steers them into always doing the safe and easy thing."

That's a fate we don't want for our kids, and I don't disagree with it. But I have another issue with the word "careful," one that is more pragmatic at the moment: It's too vague!

Remember, we are talking about toddlers here. They have no perspective on the world. Not to be a total dick, but when it comes to activities of daily living, they are clueless morons. It is our job as dads to shepherd them through the challenges without putting the fear of everything in them, but also give them appropriate direction.

For example, one set of grandparents really leans on "careful" when they have the kids. I won't call out which set, but I'll just say one set was raised on farms where you had to take care of business and overcome challenges or you starved to death and are my wife's parents. The other set were school teachers, and for better or worse, made me.

We love my parents, but Cassie and I play a game of how many times we will hear "careful" at their house, which I think is fine and all out of love. It also beats the extreme of being dangerous, which my in-laws toe the line with, given their propensity for having ATV's, tractors, and any number of other moving vehicles little kids love riding on. But the "careful" advice is not really…advice.

Kids walking towards the pool? "Careful!"

Kids about to eat some food that may be too hot?

"Careful!"

Kids sitting on the couch watching TV? "Careful!"

It's well-intentioned, but not specific enough for a tiny toddler brain. All this plus the "make them anxious" on top of it. Allow me to adjust this advice in a way that is both less anxiety-inducing and more constructive:

Kids walking towards the pool? "Stop! Turn back towards us and walk away from the water."

Kids about to eat some hot food? "Before you eat, blow on your food to cool it off."

Kids sitting on the couch watching TV? "Turn off that TV; sedentary lifestyles are responsible for a 10-year reduction in lifespan!"

See? Now your kids won't have anxiety, will avoid confusion, and live longer lives instead of zonking out on the TV! As I said, you don't want to take it too far in the "not careful at all" direction, but a healthy dose of directed safety instruction will go a long way in actually keeping your kid safe without turning them into an anxiety-riddled ball of nerves afraid to do or try to do anything.

The Importance of Labels

Kids are pretty dumb. While that might sound harsh, and your sweet little angel is the exception and is brilliant in every way, this harsh statement still rings true. Allow me to explain. To a kid, everything is seen through fresh, new, inexperienced eyes. They don't know that a car coming at them is any more or less dangerous than laying under the covers with their favorite stuffy. They are so dumb that we adults have to teach them everything to help them navigate through this challenging, confusing, beautiful world of ours. And so whatever we tell them about their environment, they pretty much believe.

What a bunch of idiots!

Now turnabout is fair play, and while I said that kids are dumb, parents are even dumber. Ouch. Thought you had all the status there, didn't you? Let me tell you how dumb we are:

We label things for kids and give them the wrong impressions.

Question for you, "Are spiders scary? Or are they cool little creatures that have eight legs, spin webs that have crazy tensile strength, and come in all sorts of shapes and colors, some of which can be poisonous?" It probably depends on how they were initially labeled by people around you growing up. When my kids see bugs and spiders, they don't recoil in horror while trying to grab a newspaper to kill them; they are intrigued and curious. Another question, and I know, I am hitting you hard with them in this section, "Which would be a better life for your kids? One where they are deathly afraid of all insects and spiders, or one where they can tolerate them in their existence?"

You can answer off the air. But this goes for any number of things your kids will encounter in their environment and how we will frame them. I will use my own kids as an example. My dad, my wife, our two boys, and I were on our last day at our Yellowstone/Grand Teton trip on a lovely hike in Grand Teton National Park. My youngest son, who was just under two at the time, was the leader of our four-person group hiking out on a simple trail. That has nothing to do with labels; I am just super proud of him. Anyways, on the way back, there was a small stream that the boys wanted to play in. Never mind the water temperature was probably in the 60s (Fahrenheit for all you international readers), yet they stripped off their clothes and splashed around in the cold water.

They had a blast because nobody labeled the water as "too cold." Nobody said, "Be careful with how cold it is." Nobody asked, "Aren't you cold?!" Mostly because my mom was back at the place we were staying enjoying some well-deserved down time, and my dad was off exploring. Our boys boldly went into that water without thinking about it, without labels, and without expectations and got a cool adventure out of it because they didn't know that they were "supposed" to feel cold. That's why my wife and I are careful not to label things as "good," "bad," or "scary," or anything of the sort. Let the kids find out for themselves. If you are too overzealous with the labeling, your kids' world will shrink while they walk around in *fear* of everything. There will be plenty of time for the world to beat them down and for them to label their own experiences. But to do it while they are kids?

Along the lines of keeping your kid's/kids' world open and avoiding the trap of "over-carefulling," let your kid(s) play with the knowledge that bumps, bruises, and scrapes are going to happen. While I am not suggesting you send your kid(s) to play on some high-rise construction site, medical waste disposal drop off, or a jagged coral reef, giving your kid(s) a chance to push themselves will make them stronger, not only physically, but also mentally. Imagine a world where everything outside, which is hard, and possibly elevated more than two feet off the ground, is also "dangerous." The world is a scary place, but like the labels I recommend avoiding, you don't need to make them perceive it as any scarier than they already do.

An example my wife and I observed occurred at our sons' school. Our boys like to run and race. Race each other. Race their friends. Race to see who can get on my nerves the fastest. One day, we were picking up our kids, and Jake asked one of his friends to race to the gate in the courtyard to see who would leave first. Before his friend had a chance to eat my son's dust (he's a fast guy, unlike his dad), the other boy's mom made an "Uh Uh" sound and asked her son, "No running. Can you show Jake what happens when we run on concrete?" As a response, the little boy pointed to a band-aid on his shin.

Ignoring the over-cautious vibes being emitted at that moment, my wife and I told Jake he could run by himself, and we'd time him to see if it was a "record time." And he took off, leaving a trail of dust and shame. I understand the desire to not have your kid(s) get hurt, but please, Dad, you who are reading this book, don't deprive your kid(s) of some of life's simple physical pleasures and challenges just to avoid an outcome that a *Sonic the Hedgehog* band-aid can fix. Instead, try to embrace the bruises and scrapes of childhood, and know that with every jump, bounce, and fall, your kid's musculoskeletal structure is growing ever stronger. You know what else is getting stronger? Their mental fortitude.

You know what else can mess up a kid's mental fortitude? Sending them the wrong messages about what's important. Confused? I'm sorry this transition is a little vague. Let me quickly ask you a question, "Are the following statements, said to a kid, possibly yours, depending on their abilities and intelligence, helpful or harmful?"

- "You are so smart."
- "You are so good at playing Legos."
- "You are such a good baseball player."

If your initial reaction is that these are helpful, positive statements, your heart is in the right place, but I think your good intentions may have some bad results. Tying anything to an outcome for a kid just may boost their self-esteem in the moment, but what happens when they encounter some life-turbulence?[31] Odds are that they will be so tied to the identity of success they may just give up trying and possibly, for good, which is why I like to encourage statements like, "You are so good at watching *Paw Patrol*, *Blippi*, and *PJ Masks*," as it increases the likelihood, they will give up these scourges on our youth.

The approach we take in our house is to try and live by the statement, "Praise Effort, Not Outcome." Like my dad always said, "You may strike out every time, make a ton of errors, and lose, but you can always hustle." I

---

31   *I am writing this on a flight from Phoenix to Newark, so turbulence is on my mind. Not airplane turbulence, but the turbulence of society's inability to promptly board airplanes. You know what will help fix this scourge on society? Raising kids to be good adults. As a follow up, I went to edit another part of the book, and whad'ya know? We hit a pocket of actual turbulence. I'm not saying typing this caused that, but don't you hate it when you get a random, tax free million dollar windfall? Nuts! Typing that did not lead to a million dollar windfall. Better keep pushing this book.*

think he was an accurate judge of my baseball ability and the importance of teaching kids to get excited about doing things within their own control. That means things like working hard, being persistent, problem-solving, and being a good teammate/team member. Plus, have you met a kid who has had his ego stroked by the incessant praise of how "wonderful" and "great" they are? These narcissistic kids are going to grow into the whiny person on your team at work who can't believe you aren't listening to their "can't miss" ideas. By teaching kids to focus on what they can control, enjoy the process of working hard, and not tie themselves to an outcome that is often beyond their control, you also teach them to be able to withstand the challenges of life, persevere through those challenges, and not grow up to be an insufferable narcissist. They are also going to work on something else crucial for future success: their resiliency.

Raising Resilient Kids

As I write this in 2023, resilience is a hot topic in my day job world of healthcare. There is a focus on the "importance of resilience" and "helping healthcare workers be more resilient," among many other resilient-y buzzwords. I hope if you are reading this in 100 years, the morons in charge will realize that it isn't a resilience problem in healthcare, but a leadership problem. But if you want to learn how to fix that, you should read my other book, *Permission to Care: Building a Healthcare Culture That Thrives in Chaos.*

While healthcare resilience is a leadership/moral injury

problem, I do think there needs to be a focus on how we are messing kids up and making them un-resilient. And, I guess since I have said, "resilience/resilient" several times, we should be on the same page on what exactly resilience *is*.

According to the Online Merriam-Webster Dictionary,[32] resilience can be defined as:

- The capability of a strained body to recover its size and shape after <u>deformation</u> caused especially by compressive stress.
- An ability to recover from or adjust easily to <u>misfortune</u> or change.

I assume your kid is not Gumby, so we'll focus on the second part of that definition, that whole "getting over and adjusting to misfortune or change" thing. Now, I don't want to sound too old school and lean on the nostalgia from the days of yore when kids got tough by working as chimney sweepers, spending 12 hours in a textile mill, or lying about their age to go fight the Axis.[33]

But there may be a place for a middle ground between the dangerous life of years past and the cushy life kids lead now. How can we help our kids become a little more (*buzzword alert*) resilient?

Give them space to figure things out: The term "helicopter parent" became popular as I was growing up

32   footnote Source: https://www.merriam-webster.com/dictionary/resilience**
33   Okay, maybe a little love for the Greatest Generation and the youngest to ever receive a Purple Heart at 13 years old, after enlisting at 12 years old. I have twenty-somethings in my family that can barely take out the trash and this barely-teen was shooting at Japanese planes and taking shrapnel in his face. Maybe a little more of this kind of ethos would be good for our kids. Source: https://www.smithsonianmag.com/history/the-boy-who-became-a-world-war-ii-veteran-at-13-years-old-168104583/

with parents who, with good intentions, hovered over their kids to try to help them avoid discomfort, be successful at whatever they were doing, thereby ruining the values of hard work and independence. Plus, the term "helicopter parent" ruins one of the coolest inventions of humanity: helicopters! Our neighbor was an Army helicopter pilot, but she also lets her daughter, who is the same age as Jake, figure things out on her own rather than hover over her. My guess is she had enough flying Blackhawks that she didn't want to take her work home. It's kind of like how I ignore drug labels and take whatever pills I feel like after a hard day at the pharmacy. And before you call CPS, this is a joke, so lighten up.

Stuck in my observation and praise of our awesome neighbor/helicopter pilot was the point I was trying to get at: give your little ones space to figure out their challenges. It's those well-intentioned parental instincts that make you want to swoop in when your kid is struggling. Trust me, it's hard to watch them struggle with whatever it is they are doing, from building a Lego house, to cutting their own food, to tying their shoes on their own. Unless they have been in a cranky mood all day, then I say let em' struggle! But two things happen when you step in to fix everything:

1) They come to expect and rely on you, which will make for long, exhausting days.
2) They never gain a sense of pride after figuring out hard shit.

Some of my proudest Dad moments have come when my oldest, after struggling with something, finally figures it out. His face beams with pride, he smiles, and in a world where both my sons are "Mommy's Boys," he wants *me* to come see what he has achieved. And with each small task that you let your kid struggle with and figure out, their confidence builds up. So when the really hard stuff comes up later in life, they won't come running to you, but instead, they will have developed their own agency.

Speaking of their own agency, another way to make your kids tough and resilient is to give them responsibilities. People and kids will surprise you with how they can rise to the challenges you put before them. Not to surprise you with the lack of initiative when presented with no challenges, I am not saying your three-year-old should be put in charge of cleaning your gun(s), cleaning your pool, or cleaning the bottom of your car. All of these would be needlessly dangerous. But cleaning up their toys? That is a responsibility they can start to handle pretty early. Our two-year-old knows he needs to pick up after himself and his toys.

For Jake, at four years old, we have tasked him with putting his laundry away, sorting out the silverware when it's clean in the dishwasher, and keeping his toys and room neat and tidy. Some hardcore responsibility givers would scoff that these are not tough enough. While some hardcore anti-responsibility givers scoff that we give him anything to do at all. You gotta know your kid, but know this: if you don't give them any responsibility to own, early in life, it will probably be harder to get them to do anything later in life. You are the dad. Set the tone so your kids know that they will have expectations beyond sleeping in, eating all day, and burying their faces in a tablet.

Why does any of this stuff matter? Why should raising tough, resilient kids be important for you, Dad? Because, and I hope you are ready for me to blow your mind: you aren't raising kids.

What?!

You are raising adults.

As much fun as dressing your baby up in cute clothes, getting your toddler to parrot your college's fight song, or seeing how big a mess they can make when eating spaghetti, at the end of the day, your goal should ultimately be to raise successful grown-ups.

If you are sensing a possible tension, I feel it, too. On the one hand, I want my kids to have an awesome childhood. I want them to have fun, make friends, and have amazing experiences. But on the other hand, all of these experiences should ultimately be funneling towards the goal of preparing them for the "Real World." We know as adults, the real world can be harsh, sad, and like most of us in employment, painfully boring.

Your kid(s) will have plenty of time for bad breakups, tragic events, and unfulfilling employment. So to overburden them with your crap is unfair and unproductive. But I think there is a nice balance to strike in challenging them while making their childhood(s) fun and engaging: the extremes are a borderline abusive childhood or a marshmallowy, soft childhood that never challenges them.

How will you know if you are doing it right?

I guess we'll find out when they turn 18, won't we?

Chapter 19

Remember Who the Adult Is (It's You)

I hope you have been able to see that I love my kids, and I want the best for them. My guess is that you do as well for your own kid(s). That's great. But I have noticed that we have gotten very "kid's rule" centric in society in the name of keeping them happy. While noble, I don't think putting kids in the driver's seat for many of life's choices is a good thing. Their feet can't even hit the pedals. Plus, have you ever read *Lord of the Flies?*[34]

This "kid think" has also crept into adults, specifically my generation of Millennials. We are super nostalgic. I mean, while we made fun of our parents for talking

---

34   In short *Lord of the Flies* is a book that tells the tale of a group of young boys stuck on a deserted island that eventually turns violent since there are no grown-ups to supervise.

about how great the 1970s were, there is no stopping someone raised in the '90s from espousing how magical a decade it was.[35] Like, I enjoyed the show *Full House*, but was there a need for a reboot of it? It is just a marker of adults in my generation who haven't really grown up. Want proof? Observe how often "grown-ups" are proud of normal activities like paying bills, washing their car, and performing basic house maintenance under the umbrella of "adulting."

Anyways, I have a few suggestions to make sure you act like an adult, your kid gets treated like a kid, and we can all live a happier, more sane life rather than blurring the lines of adulthood and childhood.

Putting Kids in Their Place

"Wow, Cory, that header seems kind of harsh."

I can see why you'd make that assumption. Have no fear; it has nothing to do with physical violence. Just a little emotional pecking order highlighted by a couple of food-related anecdotes. "Putting kids in their place" just means reminding them who the adult is (that's you) and who is in charge (that's you too), and who gets to appreciate the "adult" things in life (that's you as well).

The first rule is: Kids get the drumsticks, Adults get the thighs. If you are vegetarian or vegan, you may want to skip this section and several of the recipe suggestions at the end of the book. For those carnivorous dads amongst me, read on!

---

35   *Because it was. The 1970s included a lime green and burnt orange monstrosity of disco, gas shortages, and cocaine.*

Who doesn't love a delicious chicken dinner?! I mean, it's literally meant for winner, winners. I am an air fryer or "baked 'til the skin is crispy" kind of guy. And when the different parts of the chicken are cooked, there is clearly a pecking order (pun intended) of pieces. The breast is fine, but if a little dry, it is still the leanest source of protein. The wings are meant to be separated, tossed, and sauced as the fine folks in Buffalo intended. This leaves us with a couple of more parts: the drumsticks and the thighs. Drumsticks are fun. They have a cool name. Hey, they even come with a handle, which is to say, they distract us from the fact that it's the least desirable meat on the chicken. Still, it's the chewiest, the skin doesn't crisp as well, and they just don't taste as satisfying. Ah, but those thighs! When you cook the skin-on chicken thighs just right, it is a culinary delight.

That is why I recoil in horror when the two options are available, adults and kids are eating, and an adult dares give a kid a thigh. You know why?

THEY AREN'T OLD ENOUGH TO KNOW THE DIFFERENCE!

Half the time, they cover it up with ranch (see the appendix for a yummy recipe), ketchup, or any other sauce. They don't know what they are missing out on! Plus, they can have fun with the drumstick because "it's a fun handle."

I want you to know I love my kids, but I know their culinary enjoyment limitations. Also, you are the adult; treat yourself to something better, which brings up a story from the Christmas past.

My mother makes an outstanding prime rib roast every Christmas, which is even more impressive considering she is the Jewish parent of my mom and dad. That's some marital dedication. Also, I think there is a level of feeling she missed out on Christmas for years as a nice Jewish girl. Anyways, this past Christmas, we were in the middle of another of her delectable roasts, which my kids were gobbling up. While I was glad they were eating, I was not thrilled at the 15-dollar-a-pound taste they were developing. Regardless, my four-year-old wanted another piece, which my wife lovingly, yet mindlessly, gave him. To my shock and horror, she picked up the end piece.

The end piece!

The piece with the most seasoning, flavor, and goodness on an overall incredible roast was going to the booger-eating and off-the-floor-tasting toddler (sorry, Jake, it's true). At that point, I had to put a stop to this madness. I am not saying I ruined Christmas dinner, but my entire family got an earful about the lack of appreciation from toddlers for the difference in a middle vs. end piece, how it relates to chicken part distribution, and a diatribe on how, while we can love our kids, the adults are in charge.

Maybe you won't be so militant about the meat in your house, but when we cook steaks, we also make hamburgers for the kids. You know why? They are just as happy, and the hamburgers are at a fraction of the cost compared to steak in general. If you can find a way to feed your kids that keeps them, you, and your wallet happy, go for it. But remember that when it comes time for that end piece, who it is that worked so hard to pay for it.

The food example is just a reminder that our kids are just that: *kids*. My goal is to preserve their sweet innocence and childhood as long as possible. Along those lines, I'll bring up something possibly more controversial than what to feed them: politics.

If you think I am going to take sides, you are certifiably insane. This book is meant to be a fun, funny, useful guide to being a better dad, not a political manifesto, which is good because your four-year-old doesn't give a shit about politics and I am here to remind you of that. When "your candidate" doesn't win the election, don't take it out on your kid(s). If they still get to play Legos and pick their boogers, odds are that they'll be pretty content whether it's a Republican, Democrat, or Libertarian in office. They will have their whole adult life to worry about politics. Let them have these precious years of freedom from having to worry about that.

The infusion of politics into dadding can also bleed into a topic that may be the most divisive of the book: social media.

I will try to keep this brief: We don't put our kids on social media.

There ya go, wrapped that up nicely and quickly!

Okay, I'll expand upon that. But first of all, I don't judge you if you post pictures, videos and whatever else the hell you want to share of the minor(s) you are in charge of, out there for strangers to see.[36] It's super fun to show them being born, taking their first steps, or throwing tantrums

---

36   *It sounds a little different when you put it that way, eh?*

that are so bad, it's cute. Your family and friends can see it, like it, comment on how beautiful your kids are. Your dopamine spikes, making you feel good, and tempting you to put that next picture or video up to share.

I get it; it feels good. But I think there are some serious downsides to all the posting. Firstly, I don't like how it takes you out of the moment with your kids. I am going to touch on how you can document your memories in a more private manner. But every moment of time you are snapping, cropping, editing, tagging, then going back to and looking at the responses, is a moment you are not spending with your kid(s). It is time literally spent in a fake digital world instead of the real world with your kid(s). While I am not quite Clint Eastwood, yelling at kids to get off my lawn, I know I sound old and out of touch. I accept *that* like I accept that social media is not going anywhere.

But beyond losing the moments, I fear how normalizing it is because posting your life for others to see will affect your kid(s). I don't know what the research says. This book was written from my experience and "gut fatherly instinct," after all! But I have observed kids of families who do a lot of posting, and there is a disturbing trend of kids demanding to see what the pictures and comments say. Maybe more disturbing is the conditioning of kids and, if I am being honest, girls to learn to pose for the camera early and often in life. As a dad of a girl now, I am going to work hard not to instill the "world is watching what you look like and do at every moment" mindset in her. Same goes for my boys, I guess. But right now, they are doing just fine, spending their time wrestling and generally beating the shit out of each other, enjoying life enough not to notice much else outside of their own little world.

There is also the concern of what digital footprint your kid(s) will have, especially starting at the age of "posted pics from the ultrasound." I am not some dystopian anti-technology conspiracy theorist, but I don't imagine having digital images of your kids owned by some third-party is the best practice. Also, this chapter is about you being the adult and what it says when you can't just be excited for your kid in that moment, especially as they do something cool. Instead, you feel the need to post it on the internet for strangers' validation? It's not a judgment, but more of a philosophical analysis. Trust me, I have wanted to share so much of the cool crap my kids have done, mostly sports-related. But I refrained, and I told Cassie, "IF we were 'post on the internet' kind of people…that would have been shared." She laughs. Agrees; we send it via text to our friends and family and move on.

I mentioned I am not dystopian, but my wife and I are a bit neurotic when it comes to pictures of our kids. When at birthday parties and other public kid events that parents are taking pictures with our kids included, we ask them not to post them on or send them to any of their channels. In fact, we have seen some sneak through and ask them to take the pictures down. When we do it, we acknowledge our craziness as politely as possible, and people are receptive to our wishes. At least to our faces. They could be talking behind our backs, and I don't really care. If our kids are going to be unleashed on Instagram and Facebook, Mom and Dad are going to be the ones sending it out.

Now, you may be wondering why I am letting the world see my children's photographs in my book when my wife and I so kindly ask others not to post them on their private social media? The point isn't where they are posted or who sees them; the point here is that I, as the dad, have a say in where I want my children's photographs to appear, and it is respectful to ask a parent, "Is it okay if I post this photograph of my Jimmie playing with your Katie, on my personal social media account?"

On the other hand, while I can see the upside of the argument, "Family and friends can see the pictures," I struggle with any other possible upside. And don't give me an argument that "It's too hard to share otherwise." Here are a few suggestions on how to share (outside of social media) off the top of my head:

- Text message
- Email
- Print and send
- Digital picture frame
- Google Drive sharing
- Apple shared album
- WhatsApp

That's seven solutions for you right there. And we all know seven is a lucky number.

Now, I can hear you calling me a hypocrite because, "Cory, you have pictures of your kids in this very book!" You are correct. The difference is that my kids are being compensated for their images in this book. When someone sees a picture of your kid publicly posted on Facebook, a bunch of advertisers and shareholders get paid. The use of family images in this book was very intentional and actually, came after a lot of nuanced discussions with my wife. It wasn't a choice we made lightly or easily, but ultimately thought it was the best choice for the book.

As I have said earlier, you make your own choice on how you want your kid(s) and you to lead your digital lives. I won't judge, but I figured that since this is a book on being a dad, I should share that slice of fatherly advice.

Therefore, I wanted to end with a couple of quick "You are the adult" reminders to wrap this chapter up:

- **Vacations**: Remember when you went on a trip with your family, and you just had fun? Remember who planned and executed that trip? Your parents. Guess who you are now? The parent. I am not saying vacations can't be fun, but don't expect the non-stop funfests you had growing up. You plan them. You pay for them. You are responsible for your kid(s). A few years ago, we visited Old Forge, NY, and The Enchanted Forest Water Safari. It was the site of many family vacations as a kid and, in fact, a place my wife and I visited in our year turning 30 in 2016 as kid-free adults. It was just as fun for us 30-year-olds as it had been for us when we were 10 years old. Yet coming with our three-year-old and one-year-old was a totally different experience. It was still fun, watching them discover the magic of the waterpark. But my wife and I did two non-kid water slides together the entire three-hour trip, thanks to my parents watching the boys for a few minutes. I only tell this to you to help manage vacation expectations. And to suggest working in as many "kid-free" trips as possible.

- **If you can't not be upset, just walk away:** Your kid(s) will push your buttons and make you angry. I can almost guarantee it. What they can't really do is comprehend a sophisticated argument and explanation as to why all they have done has been inappropriate and made you livid. There is a time and place to invoke the loud "Dad Voice." I like to save mine for situations that involve safety and deliberate harm-intended circumstances, usually to their sibling(s). Remember, you are the adult. If you can't not be super upset, just walk away. Be angry, but walk away. Have consequences after you have cooled down. But don't be afraid to walk away. I have used the words, "I am really upset with you right now, but I just need to walk away for a minute. I will come back, and we'll talk about this."

With young kids, there are really no winners in a shouting match. For that matter, does anyone ever really win a shouting match? Be the grown-up. Walk away and avoid saying or doing something that you will regret.

It's the adult thing to do.

Chapter 20

It's Not IF but HOW You'll Screw Them Up

ook at you go! You're reading a "parenting" book, preparing to be, or working towards being a better Dad. And you are kind enough to think that I am the one to help get you there. Go you!

However, if you think you will be perfect, you are wrong, and that's okay. There are literally no perfect dads. You know how I know that?

You ever meet a perfect kid?

Okay, so maybe you have met a freakshow of a perfect kid. But did they turn into a *perfect adult*?

Hell no! We adults are all screwed up in some way, either partly or *mostly* because of our parents! My parents were awesome and still managed to pass along a few less-than-ideal traits. Oh, you want to hear about them?

Maybe in the next book.

I bring this up that no parent, okay... very few parents actively set out to sabotage their kids' lives. It's their terrible life choices and habits that contribute to the sabotage, and the result is the same: bad habits, traits, and hang-ups that those kids get to work on later in life.

If you were wondering what profession your kid(s) should pursue, the occupation of psychologist will likely be in demand for the foreseeable future.

What should you do? Short of the Evil Stepmother, most of us are out with one goal in line with our kid(s): Teach them to be successful and independent enough as adults so they move the hell out and give us our space in retirement so we can wither, grow old, and die with the peace and quiet we have given up for 18 plus years. It would seem passing down terrible traits to our kid(s) would be counterproductive to that goal.

But on the other hand, it's not the active sabotage we need to be wary of; it's those damn actions we take day in and day out in front of them that can start them down the right or wrong path.

Allow me to share a story to demonstrate the sober reality, despite them ignoring every request and command you give them: Your kids are always listening.

Jake was somewhere between one and two years old and in the midst of being potty trained when we realized this fact. He was still enjoying the freedom of the "poop wherever you are" phase in life, which for us, meant changing diapers and, for me, avoiding as many poopy diapers as possible. It's not that I *haven't* changed any diapers filled with big ol' steamers; it's that, given the choice, I avoid contact with feces as much as possible. My guess is that unless you are someone featured for a very specific fetish on the horribly misleading/titled HBO show *Real Sex*, you probably just aren't that into poop, either. If you were featured on that show, and you are *very* into poop, I say, "To each their own, no judgment here."

Anyways, Jake had made "that face" and was getting into "that waddle" when I realized that with my wife not at home, I had no other better option but to clean up his butt. Cassie had picked a good time to be anywhere but home because this one was a doozy, was pretty oozy, and if you think I am a good enough writer to think of another way to describe poop that rhymes with "oozy," you have too much faith in me as a writer.

I got the little fella to lay down and stay still while I opened up his diaper like someone opens up an abandoned closet with a body at the beginning of a CSI episode, cautiously and with a look of disgust on my face. While his diaper had kept everything that appeared to be what he had eaten for the past month contained, it had not stayed in the back region. It had migrated up to the sack region. At which point, not thinking anything other than what my friends would think was funny, I uttered the phrase with a fake shudder: "All over the sack!"

Jake then smiled, giggled, and repeated back loudly, "All over the sack!" at which point I gave a real shudder. From the poops, came the oops.

Jake had learned a new, not-so-kid-friendly phrase. Comedically, Cassie thought it was pretty funny when he said it, for which I found at least some validation.

On the other hand, for as much fun as it was hearing him utter that phrase repeatedly, I used it as a chance to learn a lesson. Your kids are listening to everything you say.

Everything.

You.

Say.

Therefore, as someone who comes from a public school and who played sports, this has helped me mindfully avoid the use of too many four-letter bombs around the house. Thus, kids have been a net positive for cleaning up my language. But it's not just swear words. You can't criticize anyone you wouldn't want them to know about. You can't complain about your parents because it will get back to them.

Having kids is like having your house bugged by the CIA (or KGB for my Russian friends reading).

However, if you think that cleaning up your language is enough, you would be naively optimistic. Google the term "Mirror Neurons" to find out how humans have evolved to function based on observing the *actions* of others. Also, as a fun experiment, in the middle of a conversation with someone, randomly look off at the horizon a few times and watch as they avert their gaze too. It's an evolutionary party trick designed to help us keep us safe from predators. But you can just amuse yourself with the *gullible idiot* standing in front of you!

This reality also means that your kids aren't just *listening;* they are also *watching*.

I bring up a story about my other son, Henry. Mostly because it illustrates the "watching to doing" pipeline, but also because he hasn't got as much attention in this book, and as a middle child, I want to make sure he feels loved, heard, and knows that there won't be as many resources left over for him after we tend to his baby sister and needy older brother.

I forget the context, but our family was listening to some rockin' tunes. Toe-tappin' music if you will. Well, when any toe-tappin' music comes on, I can't help but tap my toes. There I was, tappin' my toes to the beat, enjoying the company of my family and rocking out. At one point, my wife tapped me on the shoulder, and pointed down at Henry and then, at her foot. At first, this was confusing, until I saw Henry looking at my 10.5 New Balance shoe while moving his kid's size 6 *Paw Patrol* shoe (it was a hand-me-down, I swear. There is no other excuse for *Paw Patrol*) to the beat.

As Cassie smiled, she mouthed, "They do what we do," and it was a stark reminder that our kids are observing our every word *and* action. This was a reminder to make sure I was very mindful of the actions I take around my kids.

This leads me to Jake's bad habit of picking his nose. I have no idea where he learned it from. All I know is that you would be best served not borrowing my keyboard. Gross, I know. But on the spectrum of heroin, alcohol, and listening to Maroon 5, not so bad, eh?

I have told him repeatedly to stop, especially since it leads to nosebleeds that can be traumatizing to him and me; I am not sure who fares worse. Anyways, avoiding nosebleeds and the yucky habit of sticking fingers in noses was a high priority. But if you can believe it, telling a toddler to simply do something does not always work, especially when they respond:

"But you do it, Daddy."

Ouch.

And I hear from my parents after picking the boys up at school and hearing about a nose-picking-induced bloody nose: "It's okay to pick my nose. My daddy does it."

It has been a concerted effort from me to knock it off. In my defense, the desert air in Tucson is super dry and irritating, but I have really cut back on the bad habit. And you know, Jake has too. I'm so proud of us. Jake is just a follower who does what I do. But being a dad means they watch you. And if you have any *really* detrimental habits, working on yourself and them would be wise. This way, you avoid the passing down of whatever bad habit it is you possess and desire not to practice.

Here are some quick tips on optimizing the observation your kids have of you:

- **Help Them Develop Hobbies**: I already gave my big three examples of at least one of my kids hopping on the baseball, guitar, and comedy bandwagon. Hopefully, you have some hobbies slightly more productive than yelling at the TV every weekend because your team can't find a quarterback/draft good hitters/figure out the optimal rotations. I enjoy a ball game here and there, and my kids hop right on board...for about 38 seconds before they become bored. I don't watch TV often because I don't want them to think that's what life should be about.

The same goes for video games. I know they have become culturally acceptable, and my thoughts on that may be better left for another book, but ask yourself this question, "Is the life where your kid sits on their ass inside, in the dark, probably drinking Mountain Dew while yelling into a microphone and staring at a screen, really the life you want for them?"

Some of the other ways I spend my free time are playing golf, racquetball, and working in the yard. You know what my dad did growing up? He played golf, played racquetball, and did yardwork. The apple doesn't fall far from the ol' tree, I guess, hinting at my point on kids copying what you do? Except for the fact that my dad works in his own yard, and I work in my own yard. He was never great at keeping plants alive, though, and an apple tree would have been no exception. It's not a big surprise to me that my kids like doing all of those things too.

But before you pigeonhole me into some jock/yardwork/wannabe comedian and musician, I have made it a point to diversify my interests in the event my kids aren't feeling the stuff I like to do. For example, growing up, I loved aviation and shooting rockets, so my kids and I build and launch model rockets, much to Jake's delight and Henry's abhorrence. We cook together. We ride bikes together. We go on nature walks that are actually walks around our neighborhood, during which we collect rocks.

- **Be Wary of Technology**: Smartphones are a modern miracle and a modern scourge on society. I already lament the present-but-absent dads who, while in the physical presence of their kids, are mentally checked out while on their phones. And I get it. Those Silicon Valley nerds know how to manipulate us. I can't say my kids never see me on my phone, but at least I can make the excuse that I am "writing down an idea for my book." What is yours again? Oh, right. Fantasy Football.

  Some parents are worried if their kids don't use phones, among other technological advances, that they'll otherwise fall behind on their times. Just the other day, Jake was able to bring up an entire page of *Octonauts*-themed slap bracelets on my wife's Apple Watch. I think if he doesn't get exposed to a phone a ton of times, he'll figure it out anyway. If kids see you on the phone all the time, they'll expect that to be the norm. I'm weird, want my kids to be weird, and don't want that to be the norm for them or me.

  This is really up to you, and I won't judge if you and your kids spend hours on your devices. I'm just here to give my honest and sometimes comedic opinion on how to make yourself a little bit of a better dad.

- **Set a Good Example**: Do you ever wander around

society and wonder where all the assholes came from? And boy, there are a lot of them. Some of them are loud, boisterous assholes that treat others with any lower status like...they are a much lower status. I was at a nice resort in Florida (in a working capacity) when I saw a middle-aged dude, teenage kids in earshot, berate a valet driver. I can't remember what non-consequential infraction that poor valet had committed, but I can tell you there was a consequential infraction that resulted from it: his kids saw him treat another person that way, and will now think it is appropriate behavior. So, loud, boisterous assholes beget loud, boisterous assholes.

Now, I am not here to give myself a pat on the back for being an A+ model citizen. I am far from perfect. I guess you could call me an asshole at times. However, I am currently writing this on a flight. You'll see the geography of which below, I know you are just super interested in where I am heading. The woman next to me went to open her water bottle, and a geyser, just short of Old Faithful, shot up and all over her tray table and my laptop. In the moment, I could have gone all "Old Guy at the Valet" and yelled, complained, and been indignant. But I didn't. Instead, I laughed it off and helped clean up the water. Man, I wish my kids could have seen that.

Yes, I am traveling kid-free. I could single-handedly save this plane from a band of Eastern

European terrorists while delivering a baby and helping distribute life jackets during a water landing, and it still would be easier than flying with toddlers. Guess my kids will just have to use their imagination.

Then there are the passive-aggressive assholes. As I type this, I am 35,000 feet above somewhere between Dallas and Columbia, South Carolina. The gate attendant in Dallas had asked for volunteers to gate-check their roller carry-ons. Since we were on time, my ride was going to be a little late in Columbia, and I didn't want to deal with fighting for overhead space, I got in line to check in my bag. There were two gate attendants, each engaged with a customer. Out of nowhere. Okay, it was out of the seated waiting area came a gentleman who pulled off a good ol' fashioned line cut on me because, like, he "needed to talk to the gate agent."

Oh, well, go right ahead.

There are several other examples of this kind of passive-aggressive behavior I'd prefer you not pass along to your kids. Most of them are travel-related, like when it's time to deplane, and the jerks ignore the unwritten rule of, "Wait to get up until the row in front of you has gotten up," and swarm the boarding area six groups before called. They aren't all travel-related, though, like the monsters who spit their gum out in urinals. Do you know that someone has to pick that piss-soaked gum up?! What created you and made you think that was okay?! If there weren't five trash bins within six feet, I could maybe understand.

Anyways, you see what sort of off-the-rails society you can help contribute to if you aren't careful? On the flip side, what kind of utopia would life be if fathers modeled the behavior that would lead to better kids?!

Just think, that jerk that yelled at the valet, the guy that cut me off in the airport, and the monster that spits their gum in urinals had to learn that behavior from somewhere.

It all probably started when their dad, when noticing how out-of-control their diaper was, had to mention how everything was "all over the sack."

Therefore, speak and act wisely.

Chapter 21

The Fun Age

One of the reasons the title of this book is *I Guess I'm A Dad Now* is, well, the feeling of, like, there is not as much for you to do with a new baby. We don't grow it. We can't feed it from our own bodies. We don't have the same connection they have with their mother. There is no point in fighting it. But for the first part of that kid's life, there is just less "stuff" for us to do with them. It's not like I didn't change diapers, didn't talk to them, and didn't hold them. It's just that there is not the same connection present between father and child in the child's infanthood as there is between mother and child at that time.

Lest you think it's a case of "Cory is doing something wrong" syndrome, I have gotten the same feedback from a lot of dads who have had similar experiences. There does come a magical age as your kid starts to get older, more coordinated, and more sentient around toddlerhood. What happened with me, and what other dads have described, is that when the kids are between the ages of two and three, it's this "Magical Age" that we can really start interacting with them. Also, they break away from needing Mom for their comfort and food. In fact, what many dads have told me is that at this point, it's a relief, along the lines of "Ah, I actually feel useful." Your kid(s) will hopefully start gaining the skills to play simple games, try to catch (and usually miss) balls, and have some kid-centric conversations. In the words of one of my dad friends: "Now it's fun."

Again, I am not saying that cleaning poopy diapers and observing your kid(s) demand your wife's boobs while you look on longingly isn't a blast, but there is something amazing about being able to go golfing, ride a bike, and even cook a meal with your kid(s). At this point in your fatherhood, if you've been a little lazy and checked out, it is time to turn it around and get locked in. When your kids are between the ages of two and three up until what I guess is around 12 years old, it is your chance to really bond, have fun, and make memories with them before puberty wrecks their self-perception and perception of you.

My suggestion is that when your kids are able to utter the words, "Can we play," drop everything else[37] you are doing and play.

There are other, maybe less sentimental, but no less magical moments that will happen. I mean those simple milestones of life that feel like they will never come back, like the morning that Cassie and I were in the kitchen, and Jake just walked out after waking up, but not before

---

[37]   Unless you are holding another kid, then you certainly want to avoid dropping them.

peeing, brushing his teeth, and getting himself dressed. He just sort of...walked out, ready for school. Cassie and I barely realized what had happened as we instinctively began telling him to get dressed when we looked up and asked instead, "Did you just get yourself dressed?"

"Yep, can I play now?" was Jake's response.

Just like that, your little kid(s) will take their steps towards independence and those moments will be the ones that leave you speechless.

On the other hand, there is something almost better than seeing your kid(s) grow into little people that are capable of interacting, getting themselves dressed, and beating you at Tic-Tac-Toe. No, really, Jake was able to beat me five times last night playing Tic-Tac-Toe. In all fairness to myself, he got to go first EVERY TIME! And that is getting them to do your chores.

I was describing the transition to a friend of mine a few months back. He and his wife were kid-less, and he was pretty happy with that as he had all the time he wanted to tackle his various house projects. I was describing the challenges of getting anything done with kids around, and he seemed even more hesitant to get that baby train rolling. This was not going to be some sort of kid shaming to get him to change his mind, but I did mention a lot about the "Jake can do stuff now" to kind of get him to consider that having kids is not a total time and life suck. But then, I described how Jake was excited to do "chores" and go get things for Mom and Dad. I described it as: "He's turning from a liability to an asset."

This got my friend's attention, made him smile, and I

am not taking credit, but he is expecting his first kid as I write this. The truth remains, you can and should get your kids to help out around the house as soon as possible. I am not saying that you need to go old school and have kids for simply being your free help on the farm (although if you do live on a farm, I certainly see the financial merit in that), but part of raising kids into adults is encouraging responsibility in them. Along with the magic of playing with your kids, the magical age of two to three can help you start giving them some simple chores around the house. It's important you manage your expectations because they will probably not do things how you want them to, and it will take longer than if you did it yourself. Much longer. But take pride in the fact your kid is growing up and learning the joys of the responsibility you are trying to pass down to them. It will be the perfect education to prepare them for corporate America, or most teams that they will find themselves in.

Again, as my friend said, "Now it's fun."

At least for you. Now tell your kids to get their ungrateful asses to work.

Chapter 22

It's About Time to Take Notes (If You Haven't Already)

👨‍👦

There is a cliché around parenting: "The days are long, but the years are short." Clichés generally stick around for a reason, and that's because they are true. My time as a dad has felt both excruciatingly slow and mind-numbingly fast: excruciatingly slow, like when the kids are sick and up all night, and mind-numbingly fast, like how our oldest is already starting Kindergarten. You are going to miss the moments that are the sweetest, but don't pretend like you will miss *everything*. I don't miss Jake's poopy diapers. I won't miss fighting with them to eat their dinner. And I certainly am not going to miss having to watch their every move to keep them from hurting themselves.

So what can you do to *honor those moments* while staying *in the moment*? My suggestion is to start a journal. I got the idea from a coworker whose teenagers were nearing their time to fly the nest. He lamented to me how quickly time had gone, and then suggested every year on their birthday to write a little note to them in a journal. Unfortunately for him, he followed that excellent advice with, "I wish I had done that sooner."

What is the best way to journal? I ain't the Czar of journals, so who am I to tell you what the hell to do and how to do it? What has worked well for us is buying a journal for each of our kids, matching a color to the kid, and writing in them whenever there is a milestone, a birthday, or a big family occasion. Some entries are multiple pages, and some are just a couple of sentences to remind ourselves and the kids of the cool things they did that would have otherwise gotten lost in the sands of time. If you want, print some pictures out for certain entries. We don't do it for every single one, but if that's more your style, go for it! Dadding is the ultimate "choose your own adventure" experience, and journaling about it should feel the same way.

We also have a family journal where my wife (she has better handwriting) writes about our family events and milestones. Big things like, "We found out we were having a girl today," "Today was Grandma and Grandpa Jenks' funeral," and "Today, we installed our batting cage." If it sounds a bit redundant, and like extra work, you are right. My wife likes writing by hand, and I agree the personal touch is good too. Typing a letter, while easier to read, edit, and store electronically, doesn't have that same, warm, personal feel to it. And I want my kids to sense that personal feeling as they read it years later when we give them their journals on their 18th birthday, and when they revisit it in their 20s, wondering why life can't be as simple as it was when they were kids.

Writing to your kids is also a chance for you to sit down with those feelings of pride, frustration, and love. You may be a dude, but that doesn't mean caring for these little people you made won't make you feel all sorts of emotions you never knew were stewing down there in your gut, up there in your head, or right in the middle of your heart.

Chapter 23

It Doesn't Really End Here

ongratulations! You made it to the end, not of being a dad, because that journey is probably near its start, but hey, you almost finished a "parenting" book. Go you!

If you expect to get some closing thoughts on how it gets easier, and no matter what, everything will work out, I hope you are prepared to be disappointed. Those are guarantees that nobody can make because here's the deal: being a dad is overwhelming. There is no class, book, or hack that will make it not be one of the most challenging things you ever attempt. You can't be perfect, nor should you expect to be.

There is a lot to learn, most of it on the fly. But if you can just take a few small steps to be a better dad, you'll be well on your way. I hope this book was a good start (or continuation) for you. However, for the sake of you and your child(ren), I hope it is not the last stop on your journey to being a kick-ass dad. Because what is the ultimate goal? That may vary, but I think a solid goal is to be the kind of parent your kid wants to be like. While it may or may not be the case for you, I am fortunate to spend a lot of my energy trying to be just like my own dad. And for completeness sake, my own father-in-law.

If society could craft a bunch of dads like Mark Jenks and Chuck Huffman, a lot of our problems would probably solve themselves. And trying to be known as someone like my father or my father-in-law is a pretty high bar to set for one's self, but is worthy of aiming for. I know from personal experience in my day job where the world is so small that I have taken care of patients who knew both of the fathers in my life. Don't ask me why we were talking about Mark and Chuck, and not about their medications; let's just say that getting to know my patients is really more my style. Anyways, when it came out that Mark was my dad and Chuck was my father-in-law, the reaction was one we hope we get about ourselves from our kids' life connections someday:

"Oh, *that's* your dad?! They're so great. Say, 'Hi' for me!"

"Oh, Chuck was always the kindest to me at the base. Everyone loved working with him. Make sure to say 'Hi' for me and our family."

Aside from eliciting an initial reaction of "Oh," my dads have left quite a positive stamp wherever they went. I hope that happens for me, and I hope that happens for you as well. It is up to you what kind of dad you want to be. The good news is the bar is low for competence. But you are reading this book, so I know your bar is higher than that, and I believe you can get there.

The journey is not an easy one. There are the late nights, "please eat" fights, and inappropriate bites they take out of their siblings. They'll ignore you, hit you, and tell you that "You're going to jail" because you picked the wrong blue shoes for them to wear. They'll resist going to sleep, wiping their own asses, and cleaning up their own plates. This early season of life can be a struggle.

But then one day, your two-year-old thanks you for dinner spontaneously, your four-year-old makes a legitimately well-timed joke, can't put his guitar down, or cranks a drive right down the middle.

When those moments come, they will make up for all the crap you have put up with, all the work you have put in, and all the time you have spent wondering if you are doing it right. In that moment, you can proudly say to yourself:

"I guess *I am* a dad now."

Or, in this case, I guess I am now an outnumbered dad of

three. Taken July 2023.

Epilogue

I hope you learned something that will help you be a better dad. I also hope you don't come away thinking that just because I wrote a dadding book that I am some perfect Super Dad. I assure you; I am not. I fall short of my goals. I neglect some of the hacks I shared. And yes, I have yelled at my kids more than I care to admit. But the goal isn't about perfection; it's about progression. And when you are juggling all of your dad and life responsibilities, it can be easy to miss the big picture.

So I wanted to share one more short anecdote to help you feel at ease with any of the mistakes you have made or will make:

When Jake was two months old, my wife and I took him on a tour of "The Boneyard," which is an outdoor storage facility for retired military aircraft. We'd always wanted to go, but they only did tours during the week when we worked. It was a "want to see" rather than a "must-see," not enough for us to use our vacation time for. But this was my baby sabbatical, baby! I had eight weeks off, Cassie was feeling good, and Jake was at the "eat, sleep, poop, sleep, sleep" stage, so we thought it'd be as good a time as any to go. We thought Jake could sleep in his car seat on the bus while we got the tour.

Being on one of our first post-baby outings, we made sure we had packed everything we needed to take with us, from diapers and wipes to extra clothes in case he ruined them with something from any orifice he could excrete from. We got all our things packed, got him in the car, and drove the 45 minutes down the interstate to the Pima Air and Space Museum. We were feeling pretty proud of ourselves as new parents venturing out.

We parked, and I went to unlatch Jake's car seat when I made a disturbing discovery:

NO, WE DIDN'T LEAVE HIM AT HOME, IN CASE THAT'S WHAT YOU WERE THINKING!

But we *had* neglected to buckle him in.

Oopsie daisy.

There is a lesson here: don't miss the forest for the trees. There are little details to take care of, but don't miss the broad strokes, the big things, and the most important things because your bandwidth will be limited, no doubt. As long as you get the big things right, you should be okay.

Oh, and the last lesson?

Be prepared and willing to forgive yourself because you are going to mess up... A LOT. As have I. All you can ask of yourself is to learn from your mess-ups, do the best you can, and move on.

And make sure your kid is buckled in.

You got this!

Acknowledgments

Congratulations on making it all the way to the acknowledgments section! Let me make my first acknowledgment to you, Dad (or Mom, or other parental figure)! You are actively trying to get better, which means you are on the path to being a solid, if not spectacular, dad. Raising a kid or kids and writing a book have a lot in common: They both take a lot of time, effort, and tears. But a book has never talked back to me. And I don't like audiobooks, so your experience may differ. One other way books and raising kids are similar is that it truly "takes a village." So I'd like to acknowledge the people that helped me "raise" this book:

First of all, I have to thank Janan Sarwar and her editorial and production team at Global Bookshelves International. Parenting advice can be controversial, and taking on a comedy angle is even more daring. Thank you for helping me bring this book to life.

To the editors who helped mold, shape, and ultimately get the finished product you read today, thank you. A big thanks to Rumki Chowdhury for your fantastic initial review and recommendations. Your vision helped shape this book in a way I could not even have fathomed (for the better, of course!).

I have to give a thank you to Alex Barker, who has helped me forge a non-traditional path as a pharmacist/writer/comedian/speaker. Is that the order we settled on?

Let's talk about it on another Friday morning call while I walk with a rucksack and you are just waking up, even though you are a time zone ahead of me.

A special thanks to Brian Bisher, who has taken what was a chance appearance on a podcast and turned it into a full-fledged friendship and support system. You are an incredible dad and friend. We still haven't had a chance to watch the Cubs destroy the Reds in person, and it's only getting tougher as our families get bigger, but we will make it happen.

To my unofficial editor and comedic confidant, Scott Keith. Thank you for making sure that if my content isn't the funniest, it is at least not embarrassing. Sharing time with you, Kendra, Miles, and Charlotte is one of life's greatest treats. "Very much now."

Believing you have an idea for a book is the first step in actually writing one. Thanks to Josh and Victoria Field for being such an incredible source of inspiration and friendship in our lives. Our tales of parenting challenges were the seed of ideas that got this book going. We are so lucky you chose Tucson in 2020, and even luckier, we get to share the bond of parenthood with you.

Where would I be without you, Kendrick? I literally text you more than I text Cassie. You are such a unique and special human being, and two time zones can't keep us from swapping dad stories. Thanks for always being there to listen. Let's not wait another two years to see each other in person again, eh?

Becoming a dad can be a shock. But hearing someone is becoming a dad is sometimes the biggest surprise, and to you, TJ, it was one of the happiest surprises. We are officially girl dads now. We've come a long way from baseball card shows, throwing ketchup packets at UPS trucks, and having my dad tie our ties for prom. I guess *you're* a dad now, too. Let's see who is the first of us to get thrown out of one of our daughter's softball games for arguing with the umps. My money's on you. And to Rose, thank you for convincing TJ to join us in parenthood. You missed your calling as a lawyer by making a convincing argument like that.

The joy of fatherhood is heightened when it's shared. Thanks to the Manthers, who, like me, have a taste for older women. To Garrett, Jess, and Taylor, thanks for being about the most kick-ass neighbors, friends, and fellow dads a guy could ever hope for. Garrett, thanks for planning and helping execute nearly all of our projects. Taylor, I don't know if I really am that funny, but you laugh at all my jokes nonetheless. Jess, thanks for the rucks and the inspiration for the title of this book. I got some jerky cooking for you as we speak, boys, don't worry.

And there wouldn't be a pack of Manthers without the Casas Adobes Cougar club. To Caitlin, Jess, Sarah, and, of course, Cassie, thanks for being the best group of mothers any bunch of dads could ask for. We all outkicked our coverage with you.

To Peggy, my mother-in-law, and Janis, my mom, thanks for being such amazing grandmothers to our kids! They love you so much, and I do too. We appreciate everything you have done to help us when Cassie and I need a night, an afternoon, or a full weekend. Also, thanks for putting up with our dads.

To Chuck Huffman, my father-in-law, thank you for raising Cassie to be so tough, strong, and independent-minded. I am so lucky to have married into your family, and I hope I have taken care of your daughter (not that she needs it) as well as you could have hoped. I know that when I first met you, I didn't cook with charcoal, but thanks for looking past that and welcoming me into your family anyways. Also, thanks for bringing your tractor over whenever we ask.

What was this book about? Oh ya, Dads. Man, did I hit the lottery when I got Mark Jenks as my dad? Pops, thanks for everything. That's vague and doesn't do justice for all you did for me. Thanks for wearing all those curveballs in the dirt off your shins and for all the rounds of batting practice. Thanks for trying to teach me a jump shot. Thanks for always being there on the phone when I am having doubts the night before...anything big. But most importantly, thank you for teaching me what it means to be a great father. The greatest gift you have left for your grandkids is the blueprint for me to follow toward being their dad.

Oh, and speaking of those grandkids. Those kids of my own.

Jacob: You are so much of your mom on the outside, but so much of me in your personality. I guess I'm sorry... and you're welcome? You are so strong, tough, and curious, and there is nothing more I could have hoped for as a father. Except maybe that you'd sleep better, but I guess I'll keep you.

Henry: My little cuddle bug. I'm sorry. Did I embarrass you? Probably not, you are such a chill little guy, and you give the best hugs. And you're fast! I think you got Pops' wheels. And his hair. And eyes. Lucky for you, instead of looking like me, you look like that strapping grandfather of yours. I love watching you hang out with Jacob, insisting that you can do what he does. This will serve you well. One last thing, I am sorry for making you a middle child. But if anyone can handle it, it's you.

Amber: My little baby girl! I wrote a lot of this while you were marinating in your mommy, but you deserve to be acknowledged. I hope you grow up to be just like her, except maybe a little more organized. Thanks for giving me the experience of raising a girl. And switching Mom and me to zone defense from man to man. Life's going to be a lot bigger with you in it.

Last but not least, Cassie, I don't know how much more I can express my gratitude for your strength. You take on so much to let me try to live out my hopes and dreams, writing, traveling, and speaking. There is rarely a complaint from a late night or an early morning. Our kids are so lucky to have you as their mom. As for marrying me? All I can say is I tricked you good, but you are the one who said, "Yes." Our life is so sweet, and even though we are a little older since the last book, I'd like to think the adventure is still just unfolding.

APPENDIX

Recommended Resources

My hope is you found this book helpful and useful. But the truth is, there are probably other, better, smarter resources than yours truly, to help take your dadding abilities to the next level and help raise your kid(s). To that end, I have a few resources listed that have helped me in multiple facets, from finances to food and how to handle a grumpy mood. With a little help from these books, podcasts, and recipes, you, too, will be crushing fatherhood and rhyming without trying in no time!

- ***The Happiest Baby on the Block* by Harvey Karp, MD:** I think this book is a must for any dad with a newborn. The book goes over how to soothe your baby, and if you don't want to read an entire additional book, just pop an internet search for "The 5 S's," and you'll be on your way to a calmer and happier newborn. And no, one of the "S's" does not stand for "Shit, what do I do?!"

- ***The Well-Behaved Child: Discipline that Really Works!* by John Rosemond:** When it comes to toddlers, is there anything that *really* works? I can say that there are many things that don't. I like this book because it is a bit old school. Not in the "go cut me a switch and let me beat you physically" old school, but in a "This new wave psychobabble is ruining our kids" old school.

- ***Hunt, Gather, Parent* by Michaeleen Doucleff:** This was a late addition to the recommended reading but has been a game-changer for raising toddlers. The name of the game is instilling autonomy, avoiding power struggles, and cutting out the yelling and struggle with kids. She lives with and studies several non-western cultures to highlight how much we get backward parenting in our half of the world. Just days after implementing some of these tactics, our kids' behavior improved dramatically. A must-read for all parents!

In case you were wondering, those are the only parenting books I am recommending! Wow, counting this book, that's only four books! Can it be that simple? I really think it can be for a neurotypical, relatively healthy baby. I won't pretend that your circumstance might require additional reading for unique challenges, but if you are fortunate enough to have a baby/toddler that presents the classic challenges, I think those three books will get you a long way.

- ***Real Food for Pregnancy: The Science and Wisdom of Optimal Prenatal Nutrition* by Lily Nichols:** Okay, this one isn't really for you, but it's for Mom. If you haven't had a kid yet, or are planning another, having the mom be as healthy as possible, to make the baby as healthy as possible, is paramount. This is a no-nonsense, well-researched, and compassionate book for pregnancy. For what it's worth, I have read it, too, and found it excellent.

- ***Deep Nutrition: Why Your Genes Need Traditional Food* by Catherine Shanahan, MD:** Think you're off the hook nutritionally when it comes to conception? Think again! Sorry fellas, but what you eat affects those swimmers of yours. Plus, you want to be healthy and vibrant for your kids, right? RIGHT?! A foundational book on nutrition that will set you and your family on the path to more healthy, vibrant lives.

- ***Eat Like A Human: Nourishing Foods and Ancient Ways of Cooking to Revolutionize Your Health* by Bill Schindler:** Okay, I'll admit my bias on this one. I got to meet the author and his wife at a conference, and they are so kind and amazing to talk to! Plus, Bill was on a show my wife and I watched, *The Great Human Race*. I recommend you check that and his book out. Bill's goal is to show how we can cook and prepare food to nourish our families using ancient methods from around the world. There's a lot about fermentation, a little about eating insects (no pressure, I haven't gone down that path yet), and even some fun activities that you can do as a family, like foraging (something our family *has* done). A word of warning: hearing the stories of where he has taken his family might make you a little self-conscious about your simple domestic travels (don't worry, we have done nothing but simple domestic travels in our family so far).

- **_The Daily Stoic and the Daily Dad_ by Ryan Holiday:** Both of these books provide a daily message to help be a better human and a better father. You actually get a two-fer on this one. Actually, each of these resources can also be a daily email, so a four-fer. Well, actually, the emails are available as podcasts, so a six-fer? Anyways, getting your own mindset right for parenting is paramount to being a great dad. In these books and emails, Holiday draws on the philosophy of stoicism and examples of fatherhood throughout history for short, actionable daily reminders and lessons. Let's be real, you are going to start your day with your head in your phone; you might as well give yourself something constructive to read.

Alright, you got your nutrition and mind working for you. That's awesome! You know what else is awesome? Being able to buy your family food and housing. Money is a touchy subject, but it's something you must master in order to be a good dad. Here are a few of the resources that helped get our family on track financially. These lessons have allowed us to work less, stress less, and spend more time with our kids. As my dad asked when I told him on the phone I was cutting to part-time at the pharmacy while our kids were screaming in the background, "Are you sure you want _more time_ with them?" The answer, even in the chaos, is, "Yes." I will never be able to buy back this time when they are young, and unless you are some sort of mad scientist with a time travel invention in the works, neither will you. I suggest you take a hard look at your finances and take charge.

- **The Total Money Makeover by Dave Ramsey:** If you have very little to no financial education knowledge, this book covers the "7 Baby Steps" to get you on your way to financial freedom. I warn you, they are not always easy or pleasurable, but taking control of your finances, your time, and how you spend that on and with your kids is worth it.
- **Smart Money Smart Kids by Dave Ramsey and Rachel Cruze:** Ramsey's back! And he brought his daughter! This is a nice book discussing money and how to educate your kids. Ideally so that someday they are living on their own and not on your couch.
- **The Richest Man in Babylon by George Samuel Carson:** This book was published in 1926. If that wasn't ancient enough for you, the book teaches money lessons through parables set thousands of years ago in ancient Babylon. While it doesn't cover Crypto, it does show how the lessons of money management are timeless and that ignoring them to peoples' detriment is a tale as old as time. Get on the right side of money and history and heed these lessons.
- **The Simple Path to Wealth by JL Collins:** If you get the first few books down and want a simple guide to investing your money, this is my go-to recommendation. It transformed my relationship with investing from "I need to pay someone to do it for me!" to "Why would I pay someone?!" to help with my investments. Like many of the lessons from

the previous books, they are simple, but not easy. I guess "The *Simple* Path to Wealth" is an apt title.

- **_Die With Zero_ by Bill Perkins:** Okay, so maybe you followed the baby steps, got some money saved and invested, and you are now trying to save every extra penny for the future. On the spectrum of "Hair on Fire Debt" to "Hyper Saver," I think it's the latter that will free your time up more. But if you have trouble opening the purse strings (or wallet strings, given the gender expectation you'd have a wallet there, Daddy-o) read this book. I don't mince words when I say a book can transform your life, but this one has. After years of hyper-saving, this book gave my wife and I the confidence to cut our work hours, spend a little on the things that matter most to us, and improve our relationship with money. I guess the question is, "Do you want to die with a pile of money, or a pile of memories?"

Meatballs

Our kids have a friend whose parents have tried, without much success, to get him to eat meat-based protein. I am not here to debate with my vegan and vegetarian friends, but growing kids probably can use some protein because that's what their doctor told them about their son.

Anyways, he won't eat much meat, but he loves these. I'm not saying they are so good they can win over the toughest of crowds, but they are easy to make in bulk, freeze, and pull out for the kids' lunchtime.

Ingredients:

- ❑ Ground Beef - Pick your fat percentage and amount. I find great deals buying bulk and making these in large batches
- ❑ Salt
- ❑ Pepper
- ❑ Onion Powder
- ❑ Garlic Powder
- ❑ Oregano
- ❑ Basil

Instructions:

Mix together the beef and dry ingredients. Form into balls and place on cookie sheets with aluminum foil. Bake at 350 degrees for approximately 15 minutes or so. Cut them in half to make sure they are done. And so you can taste them for quality control.

Dad's Beef Jerky

Jerky is full of protein, an easy on-the-go snack, and is crazy expensive. So I make my own.

As an added bonus, there's no added sugar. I use an air fryer on its dehydrator setting, so this is what the directions are for Dad's Beef Jerky, but if you have a dehydrator, follow the instructions for making beef jerky. I typically use London Broil, as it's often on sale. Can you detect a theme? I'm cheap. But I have used sirloin as well. I have even sliced up extra chicken, marinated it, and made chicken jerky. It's a jerky "choose-your-own" adventure!

Ingredients:

- ❏ London Broil - Sliced thin
- ❏ Marinade
- ❏ Apple Cider Vinegar
- ❏ Balsamic Vinegar
- ❏ Coconut Aminos or Soy Sauce
- ❏ Salt
- ❏ Pepper
- ❏ Paprika
- ❏ Garlic Powder
- ❏ Thyme

Instructions:

Mix up the marinade ingredients together. Again, I don't measure, I eyeball, and I suggest you start following your *man*-intuition too. Pour the marinade over the jerky

258

and let it marinate overnight. Then, place strips on the air fryer basket, set at 160 degrees for 6 hours, and enjoy your cost-effective, delicious jerky.

"Less Bad For You" Ranch

This is America. Our blood type is Ranch Dressing, at least in the Midwest. And most store- bought ranch dressings are filled with all kinds of crap I wouldn't feed my dog, if I had a dog.

This recipe controls the ingredients more strictly, so you are not getting a boatload of seed oils and high fructose corn syrup. But let's be real, it is still a big ol' fat bomb. Ranch is not a health food, but it is delicious. And your family deserves to enjoy the finer things in life, like smothering all of their veggies in Ranch and have you at least know it's less bad for them. Plus, it's a way for your kids to get their veggies. You can use either sour cream or Greek yogurt. We usually opt for the Greek Yogurt to up the protein content, but no judgment on whatever you choose. And enjoy precision with measurements!

Ingredients:

- ❑ 1 cup Avocado Oil Mayo
- ❑ ½ cup Sour Cream or Greek Yogurt
- ❑ ½ tsp Chives
- ❑ ½ tsp Parley
- ❑ ½ tsp Dill Week
- ❑ ½ tsp Garlic Powder
- ❑ ½ tsp Onion Powder
- ❑ ½ tsp Pepper
- ❑ ½ tsp Garlic Salt
- ❑ ¼ tsp Salt

Instructions:

Mix it all together, taste, and add more of any seasoning you feel it may need!

Diet Doctor Power Cakes

Pancakes are basically cake. Would you feed your kids cake for breakfast? Well, maybe you would if it was the only thing left and there was no other choice. That's not an everyday plan. We used to call these pancakes, but that would be a lie. Pancakes are sweet and great syrup vesicles. These are egg and cottage cheese based, and if you can detect a theme, pack in some more protein. Need something sweet? Add some fruit like blueberries. Whip up some homemade whipped cream to make breakfast feel like a treat. Also great on these? Peanut butter. Go ahead, I won't look. This recipe was found at https://www.dietdoctor.com/recipes/keto-pancakes-berries-whipped-cream and we have added some optional modifications as we have made them over the years.

Ingredients:

- ❑ 4 Eggs
- ❑ 8 oz Cottage Cheese
- ❑ 1 tablespoon Ground Psyllium Husk Powder

*Note from my wife Cassie – I cannot remember the last time I made this small of a batch. I always triple it, and they do not last long at that!

- ❑ Optional add-ins: Fruits

Instructions:

Mix fruit right into the batter before cooking. Blueberries are a big hit in our house. Add a scoop of protein powder for some extra protein (and flavor if using flavored powder).

Mix all the ingredients together. We have found using a kitchen-aid mixer and letting it sit for about 30 minutes before cooking helps make the cakes extra fluffy. Fry in a skillet over low/medium heat, using coconut oil or butter to prevent sticking if needed.

Breakfast Sammies

We don't eat much bread in our house, but we still love the feel of a sammich! These egg breakfast sammies use the egg as the "bread" and let you fill in the center with all sorts of goodness. It helps make eating fun for your kids, which, if they are picky, may help them actually eat.

Ingredients:

- ❑ Eggs (4-6 for a small/medium sized frying pan), cracked into a bowl and mixed up (add a splash of milk if you like)
- ❑ Butter/oil for the pan
- ❑ Deli Meat
- ❑ Cheese

Instructions:

Pour the eggs into a heated and buttered/oiled pan like you are making scrambled eggs. But as they cook, do not stir them. Let them cook into an "egg cake" (more like an omelet) that fills the pan. I usually cut the circle in half to flip it over, but if you are more skilled than I am, then flip the whole thing over. Once it's cooked on both sides, cut it into triangles (like a pizza slice) or squares, and use two pieces as the bread, putting your meat and cheese in between. We have also used peanut butter – sounds weird, but our kids like it!

Egg Shapes

Can you tell we eat a lot of eggs?

Ingredients:

- ❑ Eggs
- ❑ Butter/oil for the pan

Instructions:

Same concept as above, make an "egg-cake"/flat omelet in your pan, then cut it into different shapes before serving it to your kids. This is just a fun way to mix up the usual routine and keep the kids interested in eating eggs.

Breakfast Pizza

Another egg-based wheat replacement. Pizza is fun and delicious, and yes, there are breakfast pizzas available commercially. But where is the fun in that? And now, the crust is made of eggs, so your kids get the nourishing protein they need to grow strong. Plus, you get to have pepperoni with breakfast. How many other kids will get to tell their friends that? Well, it depends on how many copies of this book I sell.

Ingredients:

- ❑ Eggs
- ❑ Pepperoni
- ❑ Shredded Cheese
- ❑ Pizza Sauce

Instructions:

Cook up an "egg cake," cut it into triangles like you are slicing a pizza, and top with pepperoni, cheese, and pizza sauce. If your kid(s) decide(s) to just not like pizza sauce that day (as ours do sometimes), or you do not have any on hand, just pepperoni and cheese is great, too.

Cassie's Blueberry Egg Muffins

I don't have a (total) vendetta against wheat. It's just when I see kids eating carbs, chased with sugar and sprinkled with processed fats, it makes me sad for the kids. While our kids do eat wheat, especially if it's the wheat their grandfather grew and harvested, I don't think a (pardon the pun) bushelful with each meal is necessary for them to thrive on. These egg muffins use coconut flour and provide a little boost of protein while being delicious. Plus, the sweetness from the blueberries is more than enough for a kid's needs, especially for breakfast.

Ingredients

- ❏ 6 Eggs
- ❏ 2 Very Ripe Bananas
- ❏ ¼ cup Coconut Flour
- ❏ ¼ tsp Baking Powder
- ❏ ¼ tsp Salt
- ❏ 1 tsp Cinnamon
- ❏ 1 tsp Vanilla
- ❏ ¼ cup Yogurt, Sour Cream (or Coconut Cream if avoiding dairy)
- ❏ Blueberries (sorry, I have never measured how much I use…maybe a cup?)

Instructions:

Combine all the ingredients together in a blender, except for the blueberries. Pour batter into cupcake molds. Then spoon some blueberries into each one. This seems cumbersome, but if you mix the blueberries right into the batter, they all sink to the bottom, and you end up with your last few muffins being nothing but berries. I highly recommend getting silicone cupcake baking molds – so much easier to get the muffins out! Bake at 350 degrees for about 20 minutes or until a toothpick comes out clean.

"Ice Cream"

Ice cream is delicious. And yes, our kids have gotten ice cream. Real ice cream. But real ice cream is sweet as hell, and if you buy it at a store, it's chock full of ingredients too complicated to pronounce. As they say – the best things in life are free. But that "they" is not corporate America. Well, screw those greedy jerks. This ice cream takes as little as two ingredients and turns it into a frozen treat. For those with dairy intolerances, I have included a variation using coconut cream. I tolerate dairy. Nay, I embrace it, but I actually like the flavor the coconut cream provides. It's so tropical! True story: after our kids had real ice cream from an ice cream shop for the first time, they asked for this instead because they liked it more.

Ingredients:

- ❑ Heavy Whipping Cream (alternatively, Coconut Cream)
- ❑ Frozen Fruits (your choice)

Instructions:

Pour your frozen fruits into a blender. Cover with the cream of your choice. Blend until smooth. Place into bowls and put in the freezer for about five minutes to get an extra firm texture if desired. Repeat as necessary until desired fullness of the stomach.

Protein Ice Cream

While the "Ice Cream" is a *sometimes* treat, when our kids want a treat more regularly, we'll whip this baby out. It's similar to the previous recipe, except we remove the cream base, add some protein powder, and an option for kefir, to get some more fermented dairy in their gut.

Ingredients:

- ❏ Frozen Fruits
- ❏ Protein Powder of your choice – I prefer Whey, but have used Pea Protein as well
- ❏ Water
- ❏ Kefir (optional)

Instructions:

Pour your favorite frozen fruits into a blender, and pour enough water in to cover. Add protein powder, and, if desired, a splash of kefir. Blend until smooth and eat immediately or put in the freezer for a more "frozen" texture. Bonus option: make your kids do 10 pushups before eating.

Banana Pudding (Dairy-Free)

Have you ever made real banana pudding? I went to school in the South and made sure I came home (not one) with my PharmD degree and a recipe for banana pudding. With vanilla wafers, Cool Whip, and Nutter Butters, this stuff was always a hit. It also had barely any real food in it. Yuck. You don't want to feed your kid(s) fake food, do you? My wife gets credit for this unique interpretation that keeps the spirit of banana pudding with a lot more wholesome ingredients. I won't lie and say it's *health* food. Much like the ranch dressing, it's a "less-bad-for-you treat," but it does include gelatin which is great for you, and uses actual real whole ingredients. And it tastes phenomenal. How do I know? My Gen Z niece, who has been conditioned to not show any true joy for anything that may be cool, said this was "actually really good," and asked for "multiple servings." I had never seen her do that before. We have actually stuck birthday candles in this and used it to celebrate my wife's annual trip around this sun. It's super versatile, super yummy, and may not be so terrible for you.

Ingredients:

- ❑ 1 can of Full-Fat Coconut Cream
- ❑ ½ cup Coconut Milk
- ❑ 2 Very Ripe Bananas, mashed
- ❑ 1 Tbsp Gelatin
- ❑ 1 Tbsp Cocoa Powder

Instructions:

In a medium-sized glass bowl, bloom the gelatin in chilled coconut milk, or throw in a couple ice cubes if it's room temperature. The gelatin powder will soak up the liquid and become a jiggly semi-solid. Then, warm the gelatin bloom (about 30 seconds in the microwave should do it). Then, add the other ingredients, and mix it all together with an immersion blender. If you don't have an immersion blender, dump it all into a regular blender, and that will work great, too. Put it in the fridge for a couple hours, and it will turn into a soft pudding.

Dezirae Special

This last concoction was inspired by my out-of-this-world sister-in-law. Can you guess her name? While our kids were at her house, she had found a way to give her kids something chocolaty, sweet, and not chocked full of "keep them up all night" added sugar. My son, Henry, gets credit for a variation of adding chopped apples to the mix because he's not afraid to spice things up (typical middle child), doing anything for attention. I will admit you may want to keep it light on the cacao powder to start, especially if your kids are used to foods that are really sweet. But if you can slowly reduce the added sugar in their diet, I think you will be pleasantly surprised how much fruit can fill the need for sweetness. This is a staple "treat" for the middle of the day or after dinner if the kids want something "special." Hell, it has "special" in the name. What more could they ask for?

Ingredients:
- ❏ Frozen Fruits (we mostly use Blueberries)
- ❏ Heavy Whipping Cream or Milk
- ❏ Cocoa Powder
- ❏ Chopped Apples (optional to make it "Henry Style")

Instructions:

Pour the frozen fruits into a bowl. Cover with milk or cream and a dash of cacao powder. Season to the desired chocolatey-ness. Let the frozen fruit freeze the cream/milk, and watch the kids try and crack it with their spoons.

9 798990 258303